The Soft Skills of Leadership

The Soft Skills of Leadership

Navigating with Confidence and Humility

Second Edition

Wanda S. Maulding Green
and Edward E. Leonard

ROWMAN & LITTLEFIELD
Lanham • Boulder • New York • London

Published by Rowman & Littlefield
An imprint of The Rowman & Littlefield Publishing Group, Inc.
4501 Forbes Boulevard, Suite 200, Lanham, Maryland 20706
www.rowman.com

6 Tinworth Street, London SE11 5AL, United Kingdom

Copyright © 2019 by Wanda S. Maulding Green and Edward E. Leonard
First edition published 2016 by Rowman & Littlefield

All rights reserved. No part of this book may be reproduced in any form or by any electronic or mechanical means, including information storage and retrieval systems, without written permission from the publisher, except by a reviewer who may quote passages in a review.

British Library Cataloguing in Publication Information Available

Library of Congress Cataloging-in-Publication Data Available

Library of Congress Control Number: 2019952056

ISBN: 978-1-4758-4957-8 (cloth)
ISBN: 978-1-4758-4958-5 (pbk.)
ISBN: 978-1-4758-4959-2 (electronic)

Contents

Preface	vii
Acknowledgments	ix
Introduction	xi
1　Leader Acumen	1
2　Navigating Leadership	19
3　"In 500 Feet, Stay Right"	29
4　"Recalculating"	37
5　Lost Satellite Reception: Leader Inspiration	47
6　"Arriving at Your Destination"	57
7　Route Guidance	69
8　"Updating Your Internal GPS"	81
9　"A Rough Road"	93
10　The Leadership Journey	103
Notes	111
About the Authors	133

Preface

In preparation for writing the first edition of this book regarding the leader/follower relationship, the authors conducted an extensive and exhaustive review of the literature related to the most important characteristics for leaders to possess. One important driving influence for this search was the inclusion of "what followers want from their leaders." Of course, strong consideration was given to the meta-analysis done by Kouzes and Posner[1] in their groundbreaking work *The Truth about Leadership* (2010), which was further substantiated by the efforts of Rath and Conchie[2] in *Strengths-Based Leadership*.

From this influential information came the first four imperatives that compose leader acumen: credibility, competence, ability to inspire, and vision. The final leader acumen imperative (emotional intelligence, most specifically in the context of soft skills) was identified anecdotally by the authors as persons serving in leadership capacities (administratively or in training roles) for over five decades. Ancillary to those five and undergirding them were the skills, abilities, and dispositions that make up the fullness of the GPS skillset (which may be found on the chart on p. 22).

Our work since that initial publication in 2016 has been directed toward *applying the concepts* that form the basis of leader acumen and what we refer to at the Leader GPS. It occurred to us along this path that to ensure a balanced presentation, we should revisit the literature for this second edition to determine whether these characteristics still form the basis for examining leadership. Indeed, they still do.

In this second edition, we present the most current literature since the publication of the first edition while presenting snippets of the overall empirical findings (and findings by individual leader GPS imperative) to date.

An unintended consequence of this update, however, is that some of the important underpinnings from the first edition are not in this second edition. We invite you to return to that original work for additional insights.

Nonetheless, as this new information is presented, we hope you find the results as interesting and meaningful as we have. Interpretation of early findings seems to suggest that while the technical skills that leaders need to have continue to emerge (for example, the mastery of the use of social media), the prominent and appropriate skillsets of leaders remain much as we found them in our initial search and interpretation. Furthermore, the early empirical work has accentuated the desirability and necessity of leaders to focus on the soft skills particularly in this age of technological advancement.

More specifically, the most interesting, yet not surprising, finding of our work with leaders from various fields is that *confidence tempered with humility* is the resounding consequence and ultimate branding of leadership at its most effective mark—the level of true leadership acumen. These results further validate our view that the imperatives of the GPS skillset is *the* skillset the best leaders use at the highest levels. The leader GPS skillset can be used to assess the leadership capacity an individual possesses at any point in time. Utilization of this information allows a leader to move his/her leadership to the next level.

Acknowledgments

It may be an old refrain, but Ed and I would like once again to thank Tom Koerner for his ongoing support of our work. We are very appreciative of the opportunities Tom has afforded us and hope he continues to be pleased with the results. We would also like to thank the R & L team who always work so diligently behind the scenes from inception through production.

In this continued work both Ed and I are truly grateful for amazing spouses. To Mrs. L (Carolyn Leonard), Ed sends a special thank you. Thank you for your support from reading and editing to encouragement and enthusiasm. And thank you, Steve Green, for your wisdom and insights and incredible cheerleading. You both have been instrumental in the completion of all of the works in print and those yet to come.

Introduction

LEADER ACUMEN VIA THE GPS LENS

Nancy Koehn opens her story of *The Leadership Journey of Abraham Lincoln* most memorably with the words, "Hear the call to action contained in Abraham Lincoln's story, and get to work. The world has never needed you and other real leaders more than it does now."[3] Her admonition is reminiscent of the opening in the first edition of this work, *Leadership Intelligence: Navigating to Your True North*,

> Organizations today, as always, need strong, capable leaders. We need leaders with moxie and grit. Those who are motivated to lead, want to lead and who are good at it. We need a cadre of influential leaders who are intrepid, not afraid to learn, and are willing to make decisions. We need people in "the driver's seat" who are credible, competent, inspiring, visionary, and emotionally intelligent.[4]

In that first edition of the book, we cited the leadership accomplishments of George W. Bush, Rudy Giuliani, and Tom Menino as each was faced with terrorist acts on American soil. We further included presidents Franklin D. Roosevelt, Harry S. Truman, John F. Kennedy, Lyndon Johnson, and Ronald Reagan who each in their own way as president led our nation during extremely perilous times. That list could have been much longer and more inclusive.

We could have included Woodrow Wilson who led the nation during the entirety of World War I and who helped the United States emerge from that conflict as a world leader in business and economics and become the guiding light of freedom in the world. We could have also included leaders like the founding fathers of our nation, George Washington, Thomas Jefferson, John

Adams, or Alexander Hamilton who braved personal and political hardships and challenges few leaders today can imagine, in pursuit of freedom.

Leaders in fields outside the political domain could have been included as well; individuals like Alexander Graham Bell and Thomas Edison, whose work helped to move us into the modern age of communication, Henry Ford, who revolutionized the automotive industry, Susan B. Anthony, who championed women's suffrage, Jonas Salk, who helped eradicate polio, and Martin Luther King, Jr., who led the fight for civil rights for African Americans. The potential list of strong, capable leaders is almost limitless.

Some leaders stand out more than others. Koehn's description of Abraham Lincoln's trials, challenges, and suffering as a leader, however, reminds us that greatness can spring from the most unexpected places when an individual fully embraces the leadership role that he/she seeks, accepts, or is cast into. Lincoln rose from a frontier settler and lawyer to the presidency of the United States and became the leader who set the tone (as leaders today must set the tone for their organizations) for what was right to save the Union and bring peace and harmony to a divided nation.

As Lincoln shared in his second inaugural address while facing the end of the Civil War and the monumental task of healing and rebuilding a nation: "With malice toward none; with charity for all; with firmness in the right, as God gives us to see the right, let us strive on to finish the work we are in."[5]

While few leaders (other than national leaders worldwide) today face the enormous challenges of those faced by Lincoln, today's leaders confront challenges daily that have significant impact for their organizations. In many instances the decisions made by these leaders are "make or break" for the organization and the leader. As Scott Gregory (2018) shared, "The war for leadership talent is real, and organizations with the best leaders will win."[6] The application of true leader acumen as measured through the GPS lens could help to secure and retain those best leaders and be the difference in survival for the organization and success for the leader.

Chapter 1

Leader Acumen

Organizations today, as always, need strong, capable leaders. We need leaders with moxie and grit. Those who are motivated to lead want to lead and who are good at it. We need a cadre of influential leaders who are courageous, willing to learn, and are decisive. We need people in "the driver's seat" who are credible, competent, inspiring, visionary, and emotionally intelligent. We need leaders with true *leadership acumen*.

Leadership Acumen (LSA) is a construct that represents the level of leadership capacity an individual possesses at any given time and includes the ability to quickly and accurately assess and problem-solve in a leadership role. It addresses the characteristics, dispositions, and the "soft" people and relational skills of individuals including credibility, competence, ability to inspire, vision, and emotional intelligence. Within each of these five components are specific subsets of characteristics, dispositions, or skills such as ethical behavior, discernibility, enthusiasm, commitment, and resilience (to name a few) that contribute to each component, respectively.

Often, these components are unintentionally overlooked as a measure of leadership. Perhaps this is due to the difficulty of assessing them. And, while the cognitive ability (classical native intelligence) of an individual certainly plays a part in developing and applying Leadership Acumen (assuming normal intelligence), it is not a controlling variable. Benjamen Bloom, an educational psychologist, related, "what any person in the world can learn, almost all persons can learn if provided with appropriate prior and current conditions of learning."[1]

Furthermore, many of the most valuable of the Leader GPS constructs are rooted in the more primal areas of the human brain. Unlike the "hard skills"— cognitive ability, analytical thinking, etc.—which are learned via the "new brain" or within the confines of the cerebrum, the most differentiating leadership skills of emotional intelligence, passion, and optimism (for example) are driven from the amygdala through the limbic region of the brain. This root variation suggests not only a completely different cerebral origin, but also a highly differentiated mechanism for learning and training in these functional areas.[2]

Possessing these qualities from birth (a genetic predisposition), or having them *imprinted* or learning about them as an adolescent or young adult, is a huge advantage for the aspiring leader. The ability of a leader to interact with his/her constituents in an effective manner is of utmost importance for job success.[3] Yet these abilities are not had by all, but are more and more being sought out by top-level CEOs for mid-level management, as scores of studies are beginning to reveal that adeptness in these areas are what drives not only the individual, but the entire organization forward.

The Graduate Management Council (GMAC) in 2014 reported that 71 percent of employers value emotional intelligence over IQ. Whether the skillset is referred to as emotional intelligence as a part of soft skills or essentially competency in soft skills really doesn't make a difference. Business school alumni shared that the top five skills utilized most on their jobs included interpersonal skills and conscientiousness. Furthermore, communication skills were ranked twice as important as managerial skills for newly hired employees.[4]

Other factors, of course, such as training and experience, contribute to the success of the leader, as well. Certainly, current leadership preparation programs adequately prepare aspiring school leaders in "hard" skills such as budgetary/fiduciary management, curriculum design, instructional supervision, human resource management, and facilities management; however, these programs fall far short when it comes to addressing soft skills. Furthermore, experience enhances prior training or ongoing training (on-the-job or state required continuing education programs).

However, like classical native intelligence, training and experience are contributing but not controlling factors in leadership. The addition of the leader GPS skillset to a leader's repertoire can begin at any moment. In certain specific circumstances and conditions, this different type of learning takes place, which forms the basis of Leadership Acumen. This different type of learning is called *imprinting*.

IMPRINTING

So, the age-old question, "Are leaders born or are leaders made?" Bloom provided one excellent answer in his remarks regarding all learning: one or two percent are "unusually capable" while 95 percent "can learn."[5] Howard Gardner's 1983 work on *Multiple Intelligences* aligns with Bloom and expands the answer to the question.[6] All people are born with gifts—intelligences.

Some are gifted with spatial intelligence, others linguistic, and yet others with interpersonal intelligence. All are gifted with varying amounts of each of the intelligences. Some are born prodigies with the uncanny abilities to play music with no lessons and without ever touching a single sheet of music. Others are mathematical geniuses. And some have gifts in more than one area but perhaps not so pointedly as a prodigy.

Some leaders are like that. They are gifted with a specific skillset that enables them to lead seemingly effortlessly, with confidence and charisma. These leaders are born with high levels of innate leadership potential and fall into the one or two percent who are unusually gifted. They learn easily and rapidly learn, and develop, and exhibit high levels of mastery in application of leadership skills. They *possess* Leadership Acumen (LSA). Others fall into the 95 percent who can and do learn, but at a more common pace, yet they too possess and exhibit LSA. Followers of these two types of leaders trust them, others gravitate toward them. They are believable and likable; they are thoughtful and friendly. They are genuine. These leaders have learned how to be effective in an ongoing basis.

They have learned and developed (via imprinting) Leadership Acumen in the classical sense from instruction and experience. And there is yet a third group of leaders who have been entrusted to a position of leadership but have not fully developed their leadership skills. Although candidates for Leadership Acumen, they have not yet mastered even the most basic of leadership nuances.

These last two types of leaders (those *made* swiftly or *made* slowly) have gained their leader acumen in a different way than *born* leaders. These leaders have been *imprinted* with Leadership Acumen over time.

IMPRINTING: A HISTORICAL PERSPECTIVE

Imprinting as an act was first identified in the biological realm of the animal. The term was first coined by zoologist Konrad Lorenz in the early 1900s by observation of ducklings and their tendency to follow the first thing they observed moving.[7] As these creatures first make their way into the world, they are "imprinted" by their parents for survival. If by chance the mother duck is killed or otherwise unavailable for the duckling soon after birth, the duckling will attach itself to a surrogate parent for imprinting. The animal will then begin to mimic the behaviors it experiences with the surrogate parent.

A clear example of imprinting to a surrogate parent comes in the movie *Fly Away Home*.[8] In the screen adaption of the book *Father Goose* by Bill Lishman, goslings are orphaned when the mother goose is killed.[9] As such, the goslings imprint on a young girl named Amy. With her inventor father's help, Amy trains the goslings as they mature into young geese to follow an ultralight plane for their migration southward, enabling the goslings to return to their native environments.

An analogous, yet different, example of imprinting in the realm of the animals involves horses. In the last few decades, horse enthusiasts have become very intrigued and taken in by imprinting. The unborn colt may be influenced by humans in the womb of the mother. Furthermore, many of these same people choose to be present at the birthing of the baby horse, to continue the imprinting process. The process of touching, stroking, and talking to the newborn foal creates gentler, more human-friendly horses lacking the natural predatory fear of humans than their nonimprinted counterparts.[10]

The key issues in Lorenz's and subsequent research on "imprinting or imprinting like processes"[11] are that these processes occur during a sensitive period, are relatively stable over time, and are a special type of learning.[12]

ORGANIZATIONAL AND HUMAN IMPRINTING

Moving beyond the zoological realm and with the key features of imprinting or imprinting-like processes in mind, the term imprinting as used in organizational research and individual imprinting is based on the seminal work of Arthur L. Stinchcombe. Even though he did not use the term, Stinchcombe is generally credited with being the first to introduce the concept of imprinting to organizational research.

In his book, *Social Structure and Organizations*,[13] Stinchcombe related that new organizations tend to reflect the basal components present in the environment in which they were formed and that once formed those same basal elements display great resistance to change over time. More simply put, the initial character and structure of an organization and the concomitant processes, once formed, tend to remain the same or change only very slowly. This same principle can be applied to individuals independently and as members of an organization.

Individuals can also be imprinted for all sorts of traits, among them leadership. Leadership knowledge (like all other content knowledge) is largely gained through learning experiences including intensive training where the would-be leader undergoes an experience as a practitioner in his/her chosen field. And, as previously stated, although the plethora of theoretical knowledge informing the potential leader is useful and indeed informative, as are interning leadership experiences, there is another form of learning experience, *imprinting*. That is, the influence of seasoned leaders inspiring and advising future leaders by planting seeds that will actually germinate through time and testing.

Based on the above information and what we know about other leadership factors, we can derive that influences from childhood such as parents, teachers, coaches, and ministers, as well as the lifelong growth and the maturation process certainly has an influence on the emerging leader. Assuredly, the training institution was a likely influence. Experience and mentoring provide additional opportunities to incorporate new thinking and/or behaviors into the overall performance repertoire.

While field experiences such as shadowing or internships undertaken during formal educational training are valuable tools for fostering experience and mentoring, it is not until a person fills the role as a leader that he or she experiences the full impact of the responsibilities that come with being a leader.[14] The quality (i.e., depth, scope, and breadth) of those early experiences is vital to developing the skills and abilities that allow those new to leadership to grow professionally and be successful both initially and in the long term (whether in the same or a different organization).

Much of what is gained in those training institution classroom settings may be put into practice based on cultivation of very early leadership experiences. Equally vital is having a leader who by example—word and deed—models appropriate leadership behavior and shares the processes and rationale for his or her decisions and actions with the neophyte leader. This oftentimes happens in the formal training stages of the aspiring leader.

As Kouzes so clearly points out,

> People become the leaders they observe. If we want to become good leaders, we have to see good leaders.
>
> To increase the quality and supply of exemplary leaders in the world, it's essential to give aspiring talent the chance to observe models of exemplary leadership. To develop ethical leaders, allow aspiring talent to observe leaders behaving ethically. To build leaders who think long-term, allow aspiring talent to observe leaders taking a long-term view. To have leaders who treat people with dignity and respect, make sure aspiring talent can observe leaders' treating people with dignity and respect.
>
> It's absolutely essential to the growth and development of leaders—or of anyone, for that matter—that they're exposed to the behaviors they're expected to produce. You can't do what you say if you don't know how, and you can't know how until you can *see* how it's done. Without exemplary role models, all the training in the world won't stick.[15]

Almost all leaders start at the entry level. The few exceptions are rare and generally involve succession of heirs to proprietary enterprises. For all of those whose career brings them to a leadership position, there are periods of time when they are beginning the process of becoming a leader. These early career stages are "periods" rather than transitions. Perhaps, these moments in time are when the aspiring leader is "ready" to be taught.

Marquis and Tilcsik, in their investigation and examination on human imprinting, further emphasize this point.[16] In their studies, they posit there are many times when learning takes place, but not all of it "sticks." By such mechanisms beginning leaders become acclimated to the organizational expectations as well as the individual skills necessary for success in that organization.[17] This acclimation or process has been described in other disciplines as imprinting or career imprinting. In 2005, in her book *Career Imprints: Creating Leaders across an Industry,* Higgins shares that "senior managers and leaders are shaped by people—a mentor, role model, even an adversary—and by organizations in which they work."[18]

HOW LEADERSHIP IMPRINTING OCCURS

As stated earlier, imprinting can happen in three ways. In their work, Marquis and Tilcsik advanced a three-part definition of imprinting[19] that emphasizes

- brief sensitive periods of transition during which the focal entity exhibits high susceptibility to external influences (such as those with Lorenz's ducks);
- a process whereby the focal entity comes to reflect elements of its environment during a sensitive period, what educators call "in the teachable moment"; and finally
- the persistence of imprints despite subsequent environmental changes.

For born leaders, this could be a genetic predisposition toward leadership. We have all witnessed young children playing when one exerts the "leader" role and the others follow. A later example of the brief sensitive period might be the first leadership position an individual holds in an organization when he/she exhibits high susceptibility to external influences or when the leader moves to a different position within or external to the organization. It might be even earlier. Perhaps when the individual is elected as president of the junior class in high school.

Perhaps, a reflection of environmental elements might include the neophyte leader adopting the practices of leaders he/she has observed or been exposed to when a specific moment arrives. Having no experience of their own to reflect on, they recall how someone they admire reacted to a similar situation.

And finally, the leader may acknowledge his/her own limitations and choose to receive training (which, in the case of *imprinting,* takes a good deal of commitment and time). A true leader will recognize strengths and weaknesses in their role and will choose to grow to become better in their role.

Furthermore, to "undo" an imprint would be an equally difficult task; think of removing a tattoo. Imprints are very persistent but with work may be unlearned. As Semsik et al. point out,

> The kernel of the imprinting hypothesis, first advanced by Stinchcombe (1965), is that characteristics of an entity shaped during a sensitive moment of its existence can persist for decades, in spite of subsequent environmental changes (Johnson, 2007; Marquis, 2003). Evidence shows that imprinted organizational structures (Johnson, 2007), strategies (Boeker, 1989a), philosophies (Harris & Ogbonna, 1999), and policies (Burton & Beckman, 2007) hold explanatory power even when accounting for contemporaneous influences.[20]

Additionally, Semsik relates in his review of imprinting, however, that

> Mechanisms that lead to imprint decay include distant organizational search (Kriauciunas & Kale), incremental contextual and component changes (Datta et al., 2003; Jones, 2001), aging and poor performance (Boeker, 1989a), changes in the management team (Beckman, Burton, & O'Reilly, 2007), memory erosion (Dimov et al., 2012; Gulati, 1995), mismatches between the imprint and larger institutional realities (Kimberly, 1979), and competitive pressures to converge to best practices (Cockburn, Henderson, & Stern, 2000).[21]

Semsik also provides a hypothetical mechanism whereby imprinting occurs. He states that "research suggests a distinction between the process by which imprints are formed and the subsequent mechanisms by which they evolve."[22] Operationally the framework Simsek proposes is straightforward. Imprinting occurs when an *imprinter* is in association with or in close proximity to the person undergoing imprinting. Circumstances allow imprinting to occur. The imprint dynamics relate to the "path duration and evolution of imprints" while the impact of imprints is dependent upon the interaction of the individual, the setting within the organization, and elements external to the organization.[23]

Whatever the specific mechanism, imprinting is a special type of learning that occurs in social organizational settings and the learning that occurs is both substantial and persistent in its impact. According to Tilcsik,

> At the individual level, imprinting research suggests that the conditions experienced in the early years of organizational tenure or a career exert a lasting influence on subsequent habits, routines, and behaviors. Imprinting has been documented in a variety of settings.[24]

For example, consider the apprentice school administrator in training. A middle school student reports to his parent (who also happens to be a school employee) that one of the teachers is "surfing the Internet" looking for dates during her planning period. As her student aide for that period, he is frequently asked his opinion regarding potential "on-line matches." The stunned and unhappy parent of the student approaches the principal with the information.

The principal, in an attempt to help educate the "apprentice administrator" brings him/her in on the conversation with the licentious teacher. Having received a quick briefing, the "would-be administrator" is anxious about the upcoming meeting between the principal and the teacher. This apprentice is prepared for the fireworks.

The teacher is sent a note from the school principal for a "visit to the office" during her planning period. The note has no explanation for the meeting. On her planning period, the teacher arrives. The principal is calm and inviting as the teacher enters the office. "You needed to see me?" the teacher asks. Rather than an explosive outburst, the principal calmly says to the teacher, "yes, Ms. So-and-so, I do. We have a problem and I need your help solving it."

Talk about leaving an *imprint*. The administrative intern went into the conference expecting "Clash of the Titans" and left hearing the teacher take ownership of the problem and even suggest solutions to correct the issue. This is an example of learning a lesson in the moment so profoundly that it leaves the novice with an *imprint*—*a* great *imprint*. This type of imprint is referred to as a "stress imprint" as it has come in an unexpected manner. Furthermore, this type of imprint is one that the novice will call on over and over in his/her own administrative career.

STRESS IMPRINTS, DESIRED IMPRINTS, AND MENTORING

Imprinting is not mentoring, although they do have some of the same elements. Generally speaking, mentoring is intentional and planned. It is rarely a one-time event. Stress imprinting is an incident that happens at a specific point in time and can be recalled precisely. It generally is a very profound incident. This type of imprinting is very different than mentoring.

Desired imprints, however, are similar to mentoring in that they are intentional and planned. Training someone on an imprint is a very basal type of training (from the core area of the brain) and thus must be repeated over and over for learning to occur. As Tilcsik stated, "Although the characteristics of early peers and mentors are undoubtedly important, they represent only one dimension of the richly textured intra-organizational environment in which socialization takes place—in addition to factors like the economic environment, the intra-organizational competitive landscape, or the network structural position in which a newcomer operates."[25]

Whether learning in a more conventional manner or imprinted, Leadership Acumen (LSA) allows a leader to move through the tasks and interactions with other individuals and entities with ease and a sense of confidence. LSI also allows a leader to constantly move toward the *next level* of leadership capacity and success. As shared in the Preface, this second edition includes the backdrop and tools to move leadership as we know it to the *next level*.

REACHING THE *NEXT LEVEL* THROUGH IMPRINTING, TRAINING/DEVELOPMENT, AND REFLECTION

Next Level Imprinting

Reaching that *next level* should be the goal of every aspiring or practicing leader. The steps to get there are essentially the same for both and are based on a conscious decision to grow to the greatest extent possible by taking the steps to maximize leadership capacity. A first critical step is *seeking willing mentors* who are themselves successful leaders in the field.

As Jha stated, "the quality of talent and work ethic in your teams and organizations have a deep imprint on how your career thinking shapes. It's no surprise that when you work with the best, you push yourself to be the best. If you are surrounded by mediocrity, your brilliance, too, would eventually slip into complacency."[26] Or, as Finkelstein shared, "Great leaders understand that even a little bit of high-quality, one-on-one teaching can yield great dividends." Further, Finkelstein observed that "sometimes, just seeing the right example in front of you is all it takes to pick up new behaviors."[27]

As a practical matter, one proactive choice individuals make that impacts their leadership potential and concomitant leadership capacity is the organization they join. Joining a successful enterprise (private sector business, government [including schools], or nonprofit) with a history of leadership development puts any leader (aspiring leader, entry level, or experienced) in the most advantageous position. Those highly sought-after positions are scarce.

Many individuals find themselves working for enterprises based simply on their need to work. Others choose work in close proximity to home. Some, for example, born and reared in Connecticut, Mississippi, or North Dakota may have a strong desire to stay near home. It is where they want to be. In those instances, it is incumbent upon the individual to proactively seek the best available organization. Once on board, the individual should seek out the best available mentor(s) in the organization and/or develop a network of associates in the field who are willing to act as mentors.

If no mentors are available, close scrutiny of organizational operations and/or leader actions can produce positive gains in leadership knowledge and understanding. The burden rests with each individual to utilize his/her skills and abilities to the best advantage. Doing so in his/her chosen field and actively seeking to improve his/her leadership skills pays dividends in the way of leadership opportunities.

Additionally, individuals would do well to keep in mind the findings of Dobrev and Merluzzi regarding the propensity of individuals to change jobs that "career dynamics are significantly influenced by the features of the organization where initial careers are situated."[28] Tilcsik, a leading imprinting researcher, summarized the importance of the quality of the organization joined in an interview with Christensen.

Christensen quoted Tilcsik as stating,

> I am finding that on top of all those peer and mentor influences the economic fortunes of the firm you are working at can, in some cases, have a powerful influence on what you learn and retain going forward. As a result, even if I'm a very thoughtful manager and I've paired people with the right kind of mentors and peers, and put them through a certain set of experiences that I want every newcomer to have, as the economic environment shifts for my firm, the imprint that newcomers will carry forward—what they end being shaped by—will change.[29]

The clear implication is that the imprint acquired by an individual is shaped not only by those in the organization he/she joins and works for, but also by the level of success of the organization while the individual is a member therein.

Recent imprinting research places emphasis on both individual and organizational imprinting. Childhood and adolescence aside, imprinting can be seen in leader development programs. Uzzi, Yang, and Gaughan in a global study of leading MBA programs found that

> the distinguishing characteristics between students who do well in job placement and those who do not is their network. Further, we find that the network differences between the successful and unsuccessful students develop within the first month of class and persist thereafter, suggesting a network imprinting that is persistent.[30]

At times individual imprinting goes on without the direct knowledge of either the individual party, mentor, or mentee. As Tyler shared regarding her discovery on imprinting others, a manager mentioned how he could always tell if people (students or residents, for instance) had spent much time with him: because they used some of the phrases I use. "I had been imprinting leadership pearls for some time and didn't realize it."[31] Leaders are often so focused on the task or goal at hand that learning based on their actions and words is vicarious in nature.

More often individual imprinting is the result of active mentoring or as mentioned previously at least active observation and inculcation of successful strategies by individuals looking to broaden their experience and possibly become leaders or better leaders. Crisp advocates for structured leadership mentoring programs beginning at the K–12 level and continuing through postsecondary training into postgraduate preparation programs, concluding that "mentoring efforts should span students' entire educational experience."[32]

Organizational imprinting follows the same pattern as individual imprinting. It is most likely to occur during a sensitive period that typically occurs when an individual joins an organization or moves to a higher-level position in organization. Organizational imprints are usually domain specific, that is, they are related to a specific field or enterprise type, yet are often broad enough to allow movement from one field to another.

Research in organizational imprinting addresses diverse areas and topics. The mediating effects of founding/initial conditions in organization imprinting has received a good deal of attention. Lortie found that "results support the idea that founding conditions for individual founders influence the capabilities that their organizations create or acquire."[33] This information was based on a study of the financial and social outcomes of organizations.

Furthermore, Lippmann and Aldrich found that initiating circumstances have an impact on the "conditions under which meaningful generational units of entrepreneurs may emerge and benefit from leadership and legacy building, technologies of memory, and institutional support that increases the likelihood of their persistence."[34] Similarly, Ellis, Aharonson, Drori, and Shapira examined the relationship of founding conditions in organizations to entrepreneurial proclivity, from generation to generation within an organization and found that "the effect of era-based initial conditions . . . is mediated by the entrepreneurial proclivity of the first generation."[35] Other studies arrive at these same conclusions that founding conditions (initial organizational imprint) mediate many aspects of organizational imprinting.

Imprinting, whether individual or organizational, is a powerful influence. It can set the stage for success or failure (derailment). And, imprinting can happen either consciously or vicariously as well as heuristically. Leaders who seek to develop *next level* skills will consider imprinting, particularly through mentoring, as one of the useful tools in enhancing their Leader GPS.

NEXT LEVEL TRAINING AND DEVELOPMENT

A second step in moving to the *next level* as a leader is *seeking training and development* that builds and/or enhances your skills. Selection of a college or university level leadership training program is beyond the scope of this book but suffice it to say that selecting a program at an accredited school is essential. Thinking then about those who have completed such a program or those who gained leadership experience by other means, the question becomes "can leadership be learned?" Kouzes and Posner emphatically endorse the concept that leadership can be learned when they state that,

> Asking "Are leaders born or made?" is not really a very productive question. It's the old "nature versus nurture" argument, and it doesn't get at the more important question that must be asked and answered. The more useful question is, "Can you, and those you work with, become better leaders than you are today?" The answer to that question is a resounding "Yes."[36]

They go on to say that the future you is likely to be different than who you are now or even the leader or person you were in the past. Specifically,

> Developing your leadership capacity will require you to spend considerably more time thinking about the future than you are now doing and orienting your actions in real time more toward that future than simply responding to things that have happened in the past or are happening right now.[37]

Kouzes and Posner (2017) end by sharing that "The ability to imagine exciting future possibilities is a defining competence of leaders." That includes "imagining and working toward becoming a better leader."[38]

A critical aspect of training according to Pearce and Manz is an emphasis of "andragogy (adult learning methods) as opposed to pedagogy (the art and science of teaching children)."[39] With a proper approach, the scope and focus of training then becomes vital to building acumen in a field. One highly regarded adult learning strategy is scenario analysis. Brookfield, a leading researcher in adult learning, places emphasis on developing critical thinking in adult learners and usually begins with a critical thinking sequence technique. He continues by saying "this exercise can be adapted to almost every subject and topic by writing the scenario as a situation in which a fictional character is making a judgment about the correctness of how a chunk of content should be understood or a skill practiced."[40]

Scenario analysis is closely related to the imprinting training labeled as situational judgment tests (SJTs). In a training SJT, a scenario is provided and participants are asked to respond to the scenario. In a study of SJT training by Cox, Barron, Davis, and de la Garza results indicated that integrating SJT methodology into training many times led to greater mastery of knowledge as opposed to typical lecture-based training methods.[41] Nonetheless, training and development must go beyond applying andragogy and/or specific learning transfer strategies.

Sorenson, in a review of the literature on leadership development, identified nine key transfer conditions as provided below:

1. Supervisor support
2. Motivation to transfer
3. Opportunity to use
4. Peer support
5. Organizational training needs
6. Individual training needs
7. Individual motivation to learn
8. Evaluation
9. Job satisfaction[42]

Sorenson's findings support earlier work by Towler, Watson, and Surface who found

> When leaders showed support for training through their actions, trainees were more likely to perceive their leaders as placing a higher priority on training. Leader behaviors predicted trainee priority to train, because trainees believed their leaders set a higher priority for training. The leader behaviors that were important for trainees' priority to train were discretionary behaviors, not those leader behaviors mandated by the organization. Trainee perceptions of leader priority were more positively predictive of trainees' priority to train for trainees with less motivation to transfer of training.[43]

If an aspiring or practicing leader is willing to be proactive in his/her pursuit of becoming a *next level* leader, it is clear that his/her organization must place emphasis on leadership development as well. Ulrich and Smallwood described needed organizational commitment eloquently when they stated that "they (organizations) must invest in broad-based leadership development that helps managers hone the skills needed to meet customer and investor expectations."[44] From that point the argument as to the focus of training is open to debate. Should training and development focus on the leader, leadership practices, or both? Ulrich and Smallwood hold that

> long-term success—the kind that lasts generation after generation—depends on making the critical distinction between leaders and leadership. A focus on leaders emphasizes the personal qualities of the individual; a focus on leadership emphasizes the methods that secure the ongoing good of the firm and, in the process, also builds future leaders.[45]

The process as differentiated by Ulrich and Smallwood seems to indicate that there are best leadership practices that, when utilized by individuals with well-developed personal leader characteristics/traits (the personality of a leader), tend to provide greater potential for success, individually and organizationally. Training in best practices is the most widely utilized approach.

Best leadership practices are widely recognized. For educational leaders those practices are found in Professional Standards for Education Leaders (PSEL), formerly known as the Interstate School Leadership Licensure Consortium (ISLLC) standards. Those standards deal with the areas listed below:

*Standard 1. Mission, Vision, and Core Values
Effective educational leaders develop, advocate, and enact a shared mission, vision, and core values of high-quality education and academic success and well-being of *each* student.
Standard 2. Ethics and Professional Norms
Effective educational leaders act ethically and according to professional norms to promote *each* student's academic success and well-being.
Standard 3. Equity and Cultural Responsiveness
Effective educational leaders strive for equity of educational opportunity and culturally responsive practices to promote *each* student's academic success and well-being.
Standard 4. Curriculum, Instruction, and Assessment
Effective educational leaders develop and support intellectually rigorous and coherent systems of curriculum, instruction, and assessment to promote each student's academic success and well-being.
Standard 5. Community of Care and Support for Students
Effective educational leaders cultivate an inclusive, caring, and supportive school community that promotes the academic success and well-being of *each* student.
Standard 6. Professional Capacity of School Personnel
Effective educational leaders develop professional capacity and practice of school personnel to promote *each* student's academic success and well-being.
Standard 7. Professional Community for Teachers and Staff
Effective educational leaders foster a professional community of teachers and other professional staff to promote *each* student's academic success and well-being.
Standard 8. Meaningful Engagement of Families and Community
Effective educational leaders engage families and the community in meaningful, reciprocal, and mutually beneficial ways to promote *each* student's academic success and well-being.
Standard 9. Operations and Management

Effective educational leaders manage school operations and resources to promote *each* student's academic success and well-being.
Standard 10. School Improvement
Effective educational leaders act as agents of continuous improvement to promote *each* student's academic success and well-being.[46]
* Each standard is accompanied by indicators that prescribe in detail expectations or outcomes to be achieved.

For leaders in other areas best practices are less formalized and/or are (like the PSEL standards) specific to an area. Still some commonalities exist. A fourteen-year meta-analysis of leadership development literature conducted by Harrison (1990 through 2014) addressed the following questions: How can managers use current best practice program approaches to affect millennial leadership development? And, what types of leadership programs are most successful in producing millennial leaders to develop the required competencies? The answers to those questions paint a clear picture of what training and development leaders in the 21st century need and the best approach to providing that training and development. The competencies listed included

1. Leading Change
2. Leading People
3. Results Driven
4. Business Acumen
5. Building Coalitions[47]

The best types of leadership training included:

1. 360-Degree Feedback
2. Coaching
3. Mentoring
4. Networking
5. Job Assignment
6. Action Learning
7. Authentic Learning[48]

In contrast to the best practices model, Buckingham asks the question "Should leadership development instead be tailored to individuals?" and answers affirmatively that so long as two things are true "if leadership is not generic, meaning that there's no best practice, even for the majority; and if it's feasible to build a system that delivers appropriately different training content to different types of leaders. We believe the answer is combining the two approaches."[49]

Aspiring or practicing leaders should work to improve or enhance both individual skills (both technical and soft skills) and knowledge and understanding of best leadership practices. Doing both allows the leader to grow individually as a leader while making use of existing and emerging best practices. These leaders invoke the essence of LSA in relation to training.

NEXT LEVEL REFLECTION

Last, but equally important in moving to the *next level* as a leader, is engaging in ongoing critical self-*reflection*. As shared by Haque

> The most disruptive, unforeseen, and *just plain awesome* breakthroughs, that reimagine, reinvent, and reconceive a product, a company, a market, an industry, or perhaps even an entire economy rarely come from the single-minded pursuit of the busier and busier busywork of "business." Rather, in the outperformers that I've spent time with and studied, breakthroughs demand (loosely) systematic, structured periods for reflection—to ruminate on, synthesize, and integrate fragments of questions, answers, and thoughts about what's not good enough, *what's just plain awful*, and how it could be made radically better.[50]

Haque goes on to say that "reflection becomes the rocket fuel for experimentation, the lifeblood of high-level innovation, the spark of deeper meaning, and the wellspring of enduring purpose."[51] Similarly, Porter (2017) shared:

> The most useful reflection involves the conscious consideration and analysis of beliefs and actions for the purpose of learning. Reflection gives the brain an opportunity to pause amidst the chaos, untangle and sort through observations and experiences, consider multiple possible interpretations, and create meaning. This meaning becomes learning, which can then inform future mindsets and actions. For leaders, this "meaning making" is crucial to their ongoing growth and development.[52]

About reflection Reeves holds that "in reflective thought, a person examines underlying assumptions, core beliefs, and knowledge, while drawing connections between apparently disparate pieces of information."[53] In an interview-based qualitative study of work and meaningfulness for organizational members, Bailey and Madden share that

> it was often only when we asked the interviewees to recount a time when they found their work meaningful that they developed a conscious awareness of the significance of these experiences. Meaningfulness was rarely experienced in the moment, but rather in retrospect and on reflection when people were able to see

their completed work and make connections between their achievements and a wider sense of life meaning.[54]

When work takes on meaning for individuals, good things tend to happen. Based on the foregoing quotes, the *value of reflection is clear*. Unfortunately, it is making the time to reflect and consciously reflecting on events, ideas, processes, or relationships that often goes unaddressed.

NEXT LEVEL LEADERSHIP

Becoming a *next level* leader or becoming an exemplary leader, the term used by Kouzes and Posner, requires taking the proactive steps to enhance an individual's leadership capacity through *imprinting*, *training*, and *reflection*. These steps change your capacity and ability to lead and as Kouzes and Posner share,

> Becoming an exemplary leader fundamentally changes who you are. It changes your relationship with yourself. You're no longer just an individual contributor. You're now someone who takes people on journeys to places they've never been.
> Becoming a leader changes how you present yourself day in and day out. You are expected to be a role model of the values that you and the organization espouse.
> It changes how you see the future. You are expected to be able to imagine exciting future possibilities and communicate them to others.
> It changes how you respond to challenges. You are expected to be comfortable with uncertainty, champion experimentation, and learn from experiences.
> It changes how you relate to others. You are expected to build relationships, foster collaboration, strengthen others, and foster trust.
> It changes how you show others that you appreciate them. You are expected to genuinely recognize contributions and celebrate team successes.
> To be responsive to these expectations and lead with your best self you need to be clear and comfortable with the kind of leader you want to become. You need to envision your ideal self. You need to have a vivid image of the very best person you could become, achieving goals you cherish, living congruently with your values, having fulfilling relationships, and making a positive difference in the world. Imagining your ideal self has the power to fuel a lifelong journey toward exemplary leadership.[55]

When you follow the steps outlined in this chapter, you move closer to becoming a leader with well-developed leader acumen: a leader who is credible, competent, inspires others with his/her vision, and applies his/her emotional intelligence and soft skills to full advantage for the success of his/her organization and individually.

Chapter 2
Navigating Leadership

In the era of yesteryear, most long-distance "never-before-traversed" travel was done with a paper map. More detailed and organized travelers would mark up the map prior to setting off on a journey. The map, along with scattered roadway signs, was used for guidance. Additionally, on the "flip-side" of a paper map generally were smaller insets with larger cities broken out into detailed smaller maps. In the event a traveler was going to a large city, the more specific particulars could be more readily identified on "the flip-side."

In our current technologically advanced society, a global positioning system or GPS is commonly utilized for the same such travel. The GPS, as we now know it, popularly began as a device in tractor trailers and later in automobiles for the general public. Now it is a common "app" on smartphones and even on some wrist watches. This device is capable of directing the driver (or a person on foot) to a final destination while even providing an estimated time of arrival.

The GPS works by having established coordinates that are routed through a satellite system. A person enters the physical address into the GPS and then waits momentarily for the tracking system to calculate the trip. A few seconds later and, voila, the route is determined and ready to guide the driver to his/her destination.

The satellites for the GPS were established based on the needs of travelers desirous of moving from one place or point in time to a new destination. Similarly, the imperatives for the leadership GPS were based on the needs of followers to have a leader who would help them find meaning and fulfillment in their work. Credibility, competence, the ability to inspire, having a clear vision, and the soft skills of emotional intelligence are utilized to guide the leader. The end result of a highly functioning leader GPS skillset system is evidenced via the leader through *confidence tempered with humility*.

A leader equipped with only part of the leader GPS skillset may find some success; however, this leader will not find the targeted success. Likewise, if by chance, the GPS in your vehicle was not regularly and properly updated, you might not end up at the desired location, and it is possible that you might arrive close to the anticipated locale and at a similar expected time of arrival (ETA). However, if there is a serious malfunction of your GPS system, you may, in fact, end up in a very undesirable place.

A leader who is a highly competent and has a strong vision may find some modicum of success in an organization. However, if this leader is lacking in credibility, sooner or later, this leader will derail. In other words, a full measure of success in the journey only comes with a fully functioning system.

The question for the leader then becomes, how often is updating needed or how does one know if the GPS skillset system is functioning properly? As detailed in the following chapters, in order for a leader to find success, each of the leader GPS imperatives must be mastered. Additionally, as discussed earlier, this skillset (the amalgamation of the GPS imperatives) is initially acquired through imprinting.

As you will recall, the leader imprint may come in the form of a genetic predisposition, through early and straightforward learning instances or opportunities, or by sheer determination due to choice.[1] As stated earlier, the case of genetic predisposition toward leadership is the exception. Few leaders are "born" leaders. The rest of us need to give regular attention to our leadership skillset.

NAVIGATING NEXT LEVEL LEADERSHIP

So, how do we do this? How do we know when our leadership GPS needs fine-tuning or updating? In the automobile, we know new roads and re-routes are being built and introduced to the satellite mapping system continually. Updates to the system must then also be made regularly and systematically made to keep the GPS current. Likewise, the leader (aspiring or practicing) must update (thereby validating) his/her skillset.

In chapter 1, the authors share the various mechanisms by which a person in a leadership role might improve his/her leader acumen. Various techniques were listed; among them being mentored, reading about leadership, and of course, self-reflection may play a part. However, regardless of how "in tune" we are with our own abilities and strengths, all of us have blind spots.

In the mid-1950s, a reflective technique developed by two psychologists[2] to help individuals better understand their relationships with others was developed. This model for reflection is referred to as the Johari Window and is pictured below. As you will recall, the basic premise of leadership acumen is that it is predicated on what *followers* look for in a leader. Considering Figure 2.1 (the Johari Window), there are four quadrants, each of which reveals information about an individual.

In two of those areas an individual has clear insight about him/herself (the Open Self and the Hidden Self). For our purposes, the upper right quadrant of the diagram (the one not seen by the "Self") is identified as the person's "Blind Self." In this area, others see or recognize traits or qualities that a person does not see in himself or herself.

For example, as we age, we commonly believe that we are still capable of many strenuous physical activities we could readily undertake as our younger selves. Consider a Saturday morning "flower-bed weed-pull" in the heat of the summer. At twenty-five, the job wasn't fun but could be completed in about an hour and the rest of the day was "yet to be had." At forty-five, "the blind self" assures the gardener that the process won't take long. Three hours later, in the recliner, exhausted and sweaty, the "blind self" has had a reality check.

Similarly, leaders have blind spots. These are areas where one believes they have strength yet in fact, they may not. Not only is it important for a leader to self-assess, it is critically important for the leader to be open to 360/Circle assessment as well. Equipped with such information, the leader

	Known to Self	Unknown to Self
Known to Others	**OPEN SELF** Information about you that both you and others know	**BLIND SELF** Information about you that you don't know but others do know
Unknown to Others	**HIDDEN SELF** Information about you that you know but others don't know	**UNKNOWN SELF** Information about you that neither you nor others know

Figure 2.1 The Johari Window

may then go about updating his/her *leadership* GPS. This updating or growth occurs through intentional effort. The process includes identified needs, training that utilizes various methodologies, and follow-up assessment. Due to the nature of the learning mechanism associated with this type of training, time is also an important consideration. A minimum of six months of repetitive training is required to produce a fully accurate leader GPS. The following pages report that process in the work that has already been accomplished.

But first, you may ask, "how is that process measured?" A free self-assessment may be taken by going to the website at www.leadershipimprinting.com and clicking on the "Take the Test" tab. Once complete, the leader may discover a subscore indicating a need for growth, for example, in leader inspiration.

Table 2.1 lists the *Leadership GPS model* that will be described in detail in the following chapters. The skillset is comprised of leader imperatives, which are the *imprints* needed for successful leadership. These are skills or

Table 2.1 The Five Leader Imperatives of the Leadership GPS Model

Leadership GPS Skillset				
The Five Leader Imperatives				
CREDIBILITY	COMPETENCE	INSPIRATION	VISION	EMOTIONAL INTELLIGENCE
Ethics or Personal Accountability	Discernibility	Enthusiastic	Commitment	Resilience
Honesty	Perception	Energetic	Sense of Direction	Communication and Listening
Responsibility	Conflict Resolution Skills	Passionate	Professionalism	Happiness
Trust	Problem-Solving and Decision-Making Skills	Optimistic	Decisive	Personality Traits
Integrity	Relationship Building	Genuine	Work Ethic	Sense of Humor
Sincerity	Planning and Implementation	Courageous	Concern for the Future	Assertiveness
	Assessment & Evaluation			Flexibility
				Empathy/Interpersonal Interactions

* For your free self-assessment with results, go to www.leadershipimprinting.com and click on the header "Take the Test."

abilities you can enjoy as your own. You may already have a modicum of some, many, or all of these skills. You can also improve in some, many, or all of these skills.

The collection of words or phrases beneath each of the headings in Table 2.1 are descriptors for measuring effective leader acumen in each of the imperative areas. The Leader/Educator Assessment (based on this table) can be utilized to evaluate the level of skill (via self-report) in each area. More effectively, it can be utilized as a tool for 360-feedback (often-times referred to as a CIRCLE), eliciting responses from peers, subordinates, and supervisors for a more realistic view of the skillset had by an individual.

Again, completing the self-assessment is free and allows one to view areas of strength as well as areas of relative weakness. Maintaining or enhancing areas of strength while improving areas of relative weakness requires further action. And, while there are many options, ultimately, the best option for an emerging leader is to learn how to enhance skills across the board but with emphasis in the areas where the most work is needed.

IMPROVING LEADER ACUMEN

Our initial work with leadership research spanned two areas: assessing and training *aspiring* leaders and assessing and training *practicing* leaders. The group of *aspiring* leaders has been drawn from two largely different university settings that are geographically distant, and also widely separated in the fields they encompass: one education, the other, medicine. The commonality these aspiring leaders (students) share is that all of them are in graduate programs (masters, specialists, or doctoral) and all are training to become leaders in their respective fields.

The group of *practicing* leaders was drawn from a sizeable school district in the southeastern United States. The district is large geographically and encompasses almost all of the county in which it is situated. It is comprised of schools that are urban, suburban, and rural in nature, as well as schools ranging in size from a few hundred students to a student enrollment approaching 3,000. Approximately 100 school leaders were involved in the initial assessment only or the assessment and subsequent training. The bulk of these participants were school principals. A smaller part of the group represented leadership at the central administration level.

This work has taken us on a 24-month journey (to date) to examine the results of those leader assessments and the relationships those assessments presented. One thing became apparent early on. The degree of congruity between how the aspiring leaders and experienced leaders viewed themselves and how they were viewed by their CIRCLEs (the 360-group evaluating each participant) were often very different. While the aspiring leader and experienced leader scores fell within a relatively narrow range and reflected, as might be anticipated, a positive self-perception, the results of the CIRCLE assessments ranged from very positive to very negative. The CIRCLE scores between the two groups (aspiring and practicing) were highly different. It would appear this was due to the composition of the CIRCLEs.

The *practicing* administrators CIRCLEs consisted of their faculty and staff while the *aspiring* leader CIRCLEs were self-selected. Hence, the *aspiring* leaders' scores (in general) were much higher than the *practicing* group. In some cases, there was such disparity between the self and circle scores that personalized, individual meetings were seen as a necessity to insure each *practicing* administrator understood the implications of the results.

As shared earlier, the end result of a fully functioning leader GPS system is evidenced via the leader through confidence tempered with humility. This was evidenced time and again with the group of practicing administrators. The administrators in the most successful schools (based on the state report card) consistently received feedback from their CIRCLEs (the 360 group), which was higher than the average score for all leaders.

Additionally, the Self-scores of these same leaders were also above average, yet not as high as the CIRCLE rating. This Self-rating (a rating that was above the average yet lower than the CIRCLE rating) reflected leader humility. As identified earlier in the chapter, our research to-date has revealed the pinnacle of leader acumen is revealed in self-confidence tempered with humility. The following pages are shared in an effort to clarify what is reflected in those words.

LEADER CONFIDENCE

The Latin root of the word "confidence" is *con fidere*, which translates to "with faith."[3] A leader who has faith or belief in his/her own capabilities as leader is very appealing. In fact, this self-confidence is contagious; it sparks confidence in followers. But, how does a leader become self-confident?

Hollenbeck and Hall[4] suggest that self-confidence is one factor that may carry some to achievement. In their research, they found that the precursors of self-confidence include successful experiences from the past, observing the experiences of others, being convinced by others they are capable (social persuasion), and emotional arousal, or the positive feelings we associate with successful leading. Stajovak and Luthens[5] similarly found that self-efficacy (self-confidence) was strongly related to positive work-related performance. Albert Bandura, renowned social psychologist, put it like this:

Perceived self-efficacy, or a belief in one's personal capabilities, regulates human functioning in four major ways:

Cognitive: People with high self-efficacy are more likely to have high aspirations, take long views, think soundly, set for themselves difficult challenges, and commit themselves firmly to meeting those challenges. They guide their actions by visualizing successful outcomes instead of dwelling on personal deficiencies or ways in which things might go wrong.

Motivational: People motivate themselves by forming beliefs about what they can do, anticipating likely outcomes, setting goals, and planning courses of action. Their motivation will be stronger if they believe they can attain their goals and adjust them based on their progress. Self-efficacy beliefs determine the goals people set for themselves, how much effort they expend, how long they persevere, and how resilient they are in the face of failures and setbacks.

Mood or Affect: How much stress or depression people experience in threatening or difficult situations depends largely on how well they think they can cope. Efficacy beliefs regulate emotional states in several ways: (1) People who believe they can manage threats are less distressed by them; those who lack self-efficacy are more likely to magnify risks. (2) People with high self-efficacy lower their stress and anxiety by acting in ways that make the environment less threatening. (3) People with high coping capacities have better control over disturbing thoughts. Research shows that what causes distress is not the sheer frequency of the thoughts but the inability to turn them off. People with high self-efficacy are able to relax, divert their attention, calm themselves, and seek support from friends, family, and others. For someone who is confident of getting relief in these ways, anxiety and sadness are easier to tolerate. (4) Furthermore, low self-efficacy can lead directly to depression in at least three ways: (a) A person who feels unable to prevent recurrent depressive thoughts or dejected rumination is more likely to have repeated episodes of depression. (b) Low self-efficacy causes the defeat of one's hopes, and the resulting low mood further weakens self-efficacy, creating a vicious downward cycle. (c) People with low self-efficacy do not develop the satisfying social relationships that make chronic stress easier to bear. The resulting sense of social inefficacy not only contributes directly to depression but further reduces social support.[6]

In short, Bandura reports that a strong sense of self-efficacy enhances personal accomplishment in many ways.[7] We agree.

A leader's self-confidence can be evidence of strong leader acumen. However, this self-confidence must be tempered with humility. Without humility, even the once "best" leader may be or can become ego-centric or even narcissistic. Leader derailment will then likely become a factor. (This will be discussed in detail in chapter 9.) However, self-confidence tempered with the sine quo non of leadership—*humility*—culminates in the pinnacle of leadership; true leader acumen.

LEADER HUMILITY

Of confidence, Knight[8] says "be confident—but not overconfident. . . . You want to be viewed as a person [others] can work with. . . . Your goal is to demonstrate that you're someone with a depth of knowledge but who also wants to learn and help. . . . Project competence. Show conviction; but be humble about it." This wise admonition will propel the confident leader into a rightful status.

Dillon[9] rightly shared that leaders don't permit their position of authority to allow them to think they are wiser than those they lead. "Leaders who think they know more than those they lead deprive themselves of the collective wisdom and knowledge of the community. In addition, leaders who rely on a 'power over' approach suppress honest feedback and risk-taking from those they lead."

> But what is it about humility that creates greatness? Mayo[10] shares that humble leaders improve the performance of a company in the long run because they create more collaborative environments. They have a balanced view of themselves—both their virtues and shortcomings—and a strong appreciation of others' strengths and contributions, while being open to new ideas and feedback.

The key for successful leadership, as described by Cable[11] in his 2018 article in *HBR*, is to help "people feel purposeful, motivated, and energized so they can bring their best selves to work." Cable goes on to share that one of the best ways to do this is through humility. Hu, Erodofan, Jiang, and Bauer[12] feel that this mindset, serving through humility, creates a culture where idea exchange, creativity, and team-building can flourish.

Additionally, reflecting on the underpinning of leader acumen, when it comes to followers and leader humility, Walters and Diab[13] share that

> the relation(ship) between humble leadership and employee engagement (is) fully mediated by psychological safety. Thus, by acknowledging limitations and mistakes, recognizing followers' strengths and contributions, and modeling teachability, leaders can create an environment in which followers can act without fear of negative ramifications and can fully engage in their work.

Furthermore, Hayes and Comer[14] share that humility connects leaders to followers through the "common bond of humanity." Ruffenach[15] puts it this way:

> Sometimes the best source of development comes from the very people we interact with and lead every day. But you have to have humility in the workplace to make yourself vulnerable enough to ask for their feedback and even more humble to accept it. You have to let them know you are human.

Humility builds trust and trust is the cornerstone of credibility.

Skill enhancement begins with a clear understanding of the skillset leaders need to succeed. With that understanding as a base to build upon, an aspiring leader can seek out opportunities to enhance his/her skillset. But it all starts with knowing where you are currently and making the decision to move forward to enhanced leader acumen and success. The following chapters will help build that understanding with GPS analogies and real-life examples. Then the decision is up to you.

Chapter 3

"In 500 Feet, Stay Right"
Leader Credibility

In 500 feet, stay right. This seems more of a common-sense directive than a GPS analogy, and it is. Why? Because we expect our leaders to always *stay right*. We expect them to make the *right* choices, do the *right* thing, behave in the *right* way, go to the *right* places, and know the *right* people. We look for our leaders to *be right*. And *rightness* gives them credibility. Does this mean that leaders who do not wear the right clothes or always have the *right* words are not credible or less credible? Certainly not.

However, a study by Salary for Business.com[1] shares many valuable points regarding dress including the remark that "people who dress professionally act more professional on the job. Dressing in jeans and a t-shirt does not exude professionalism, especially when you are seated in close proximity to an executive in a business suit." In this same study, the majority of respondents admitted they make assumptions about people based on the way they are dressed.

With regard to saying the right thing, in *The Top Complaints from Employees about Their Leaders*, "91% of employees say communication issues can drag executives down."[2] So, credibility is not only about *being* credible, it is also about others *believing* that you *have* credibility.

Moreover, it's not just about the clothes a leader wears or what he/she says. Consider the leader who has a commitment to his/her religious beliefs such that he/she acts accordingly—for example, they refuse to schedule activities on Wednesday nights due to potential church activity conflicts. This attitude is opposed to the leader who does not share this belief system and therefore may schedule an occasional Sunday workday (or the like). Some would regard these belief systems as a show of credibility.

We want our leaders to have a belief system that we can admire—one that we believe is credible. If we have a leader who is a member of a discriminatory or elitist group or who holds wildly radical political views or perhaps is a member of an organized "swingers" club, we tend to have questions regarding their credibility.

So how do you attain *credibility* if you haven't enjoyed it before? Some of the ways to create the perception that you are credible have been alluded to above. Dress, speech, attitude, affiliations—all of these are a part of helping others have a willingness to put their trust in you as a leader. But credibility is much deeper than these things.

Credibility is a word that always seems to conjure up images of a constant striving. In the competitive, "what-have-you-done-for-me-lately" work environment when leaders must be like magicians and always be ready to pull the next "rabbit out of the hat" (the next big creation, innovation, project), leaders are often only as good as their last successful undertaking. Developing and maintaining credibility is a career-long and, more often than not, a lifelong pursuit. Kouzes and Posner, highly regarded authors on leadership, state,

> What we found quite unexpectedly in our initial research and have reaffirmed ever since is that, above all else, people want leaders who are credible. We want to believe in our leaders. We want to have faith and confidence in them as people. We want to believe that their word can be trusted, that they have the knowledge and skill to lead, and that they are personally excited and enthusiastic about the direction in which we are headed. Credibility is the foundation of leadership.[3]

Comments like those of Kouzes and Posner extolling the importance of leader credibility can be found throughout the literature. Brian Leavy, former dean of the Dublin City University School of Business, shared that, "all great leaders recognise credibility as the dynamic currency of leadership."[4] DePuy holds that "Successful leadership relies heavily on three factors, trust, credibility, and respect, which he refers to as the 'linchpins of success."[5]

Stephen Covey, in discussing what he described as the four roles of leadership, stated, "The first role is simply to be an example, a model: one whose life has credibility with others, has integrity, diligence, humility, the spirit of servant-leadership, of contribution. This is the most fundamental of our roles."[6] Ken Blanchard, in his book *The Secret*, stated, "For a leader to be successful, he or she must embody the values of their organization. So, if you are leading at your child's school or in your church, you should embody the values of that particular organization. The power is in the trust and credibility you build."[7]

Walter Cronkite was the news anchorman for the CBS Evening News in the 1960s and 1970s. He was often cited as "the most trusted man in America." His composure during the Kennedy assassination was one of many events that merited Cronkite that title. In the late 1960s, Cronkite made a trip to Vietnam in order to report to America what was truly happening on the ground.

During his broadcast, he said, "To say that we are closer to victory today is to believe, in the face of the evidence, the optimists who have been wrong in the past. But it is increasingly clear to this reporter that the only rational way out then will be to negotiate, not as victors, but as an honorable people who lived up to their pledge to defend democracy, and did the best they could." His reporting was so credible that then president Lyndon B. Johnson shared, "If I've lost Cronkite, I've lost the country."[8]

As significant as credibility is to leadership, it is equally fragile. Credibility is as easily lost as it is hard to gain. Kaipa said, "When your words and actions don't align, you have fallen into the Credibility Gap. When you have a credibility gap at your workplace, it is damaging to your reputation and to your career. And if you're in a leadership or customer service role, your credibility gap could be hurting your company."[9]

DePuy[10] related that "Trust, credibility, and respect can be destroyed in a day, often taking years to rebuild—meanwhile, employee engagement is evaporating and the mission suffering." Leaders remain credible as long as experiences and the passage of time confirm that their assertions, and related decisions, are/were in line with the requirements of circumstances. While major blunders/missteps can obviously negatively impact credibility, even small missteps can have less than positive consequences. As Kouzes makes explicit in an example from an interview session,

> One of the things I write and talk about a lot is personal credibility. Credibility is the foundation of all leadership. I was talking about it in front of a group of about 3,000 store managers from around the country at a big retail organization's annual conference. I was making a point about being competent, and I was referring to the CEO of this company by his first name: Let's call him Dan. I would say, "As Dan said," because I had the opportunity to interview him before the event. Then, about the third time I quoted him, someone in the back said, "It's David." I had been misspeaking the whole time, and it was very embarrassing! But it was a wonderful learning opportunity to point out to the audience that I had been talking about credibility, and I had just diminished my own by calling somebody by the wrong name. Sometimes the best lessons in life come when you screw up.[11]

Similarly, in a 2014 race at the Talladega Superspeedway, Earnhardt Jr. lost his track position when he chose to pit. Back on the track, the NASCAR superstar found himself in thirteenth position. Rather than making a move to get back into the thick of the race, he laid back most of the entire last thirty laps of the race. To Earnhardt, it seemed the wise thing to do.

Having suffered a concussion in 2012, it didn't appear to be plausible to mix it up in the tight Talladega, which is known for its big wrecks. But, there were no big pile-ups on this day and his loyal fan base was not happy. One of his supporters remarked, "So why should I and thousands of other fans pay to see someone who does not feel like racing. Remind me, please."[12] Again, credibility is fragile and as much as Junior's fans love him, on this day they were not happy with him.

THE IMPORTANCE OF LEADERSHIP CREDIBILITY

In the original version of this book, the authors began discussion of the leadership imperatives with *credibility*. Credibility was selected to come first as we believe it is the cornerstone of good leadership. Upon revisiting leader credibility for this second edition, one thing is very evident—credibility continues to be viewed as the preeminent leader characteristic. As Morgan stated, "Credibility is the foundation of any effective leadership style. Without it, there is no trust in our relationships. With it, we're able to influence others."[13]

Comparable acknowledgments of the importance of leader credibility are abundant in the literature. Examining credibility in relation to transformational and servant leadership, two of the most prominent current leadership styles, the trend continues. Williams, Raffo, and Clark hold that "credibility is an antecedent of transformational leadership."[14] Of the relationship between servant leadership and credibility, Jaiswal and Dhar report "servant leaders have a vision for the growth and development of subordinates through which they gain credibility and trust, which in turn helps servant leaders bring out the best from subordinates."[15]

Han Ming Chng, Tae-Yeo, Gilbreath, and Andersson create a sense of the importance of credibility when they share that "leadership is the relationship between people who aspire to lead and those who choose whether or not to follow. And it hinges on the leader's credibility."[16] Stated simply, Timko holds that "the follower, who believes that the leader is credible, will follow the leader."[17]

In like manner, Yuningsih and Mulyana share that "to gain the trust of his subordinates, a leader must have credibility in the eyes of his subordinates."[18] Addressing the same relationship, Engelbrecht, Heine, and Mahembe share that "based on social learning theory, subordinates will be inclined to trust ethical leaders because of their role modeling behaviour demonstrated through their credibility and trustworthiness."[19] From a team sport perspective, Gulak-Lipka notes that "the credibility of the leader, which significantly extends beyond professional consistency and competence, is essential."[20]

Petty's remark that "there's no such thing as too much credibility" sums up of the overarching opinion of leadership researchers regarding the global significance of credibility to leaders and leadership.[21] It is interesting to note, however, the breadth and scope of credibility in leadership research. Bracchitta describing "getting communication right" holds that "establishing internal and external credibility is critical."[22] As it is readily communicated from source after source, credibility is of paramount importance when it comes to leadership.

COMPONENTS OF CREDIBILITY

The Leader GPS model addresses credibility as doing what is right based on a leader having a well-grounded sense of ethics and personal accountability, honesty, responsibility, integrity, and being sincere in interactions with others. These characteristics are what tend to set highly successful leaders, those with high Leadership Acumen, apart. Importantly the habits and dispositions on which credibility is based can be taught or observed, learned, and imprinted. The following characteristics embody the knowledge and skills needed for building credibility.

ETHICS OR PERSONAL ACCOUNTABILITY

Doing what is right begins with ethical behavior and personal accountability. Ethical behavior has the connotation of behavior that is morally acceptable. What is morally acceptable—not in the sense of denominational religious/spiritual beliefs (though that might be true as well) but in terms of mores, the normative morally acceptable behaviors—of a given society or organization?

In that regard, Langvardt[23] holds that leaders play "dual roles . . . regarding matters of ethics: they are students in the sense that they learn, or should learn, from relevant experiences (both their own and those of others); and, through the examples they set, they are teachers of other persons affiliated with the organization and of non-affiliated persons who observe their actions."

Personal accountability is the simultaneous process in judging whether leader behavior is ethical. No leader is perfect. Missteps will occur. Hopefully those missteps will be few and infrequent. But when they happen, the ethical leader is accountable for his/her actions. They do not blame others or circumstances. The words, "that was my decision and I am accountable for it," make a difference to those within and external to an organization.

HONESTY

Doing what is right also means being honest. Being honest is itself a requisite characteristic of a leader who is credible. It is also a requisite characteristic for colleagues, or for that matter for all members of an organization. The importance of honesty is emphasized by Kouzes and Posner who report that, "In an ongoing project surveying tens of thousands of working people around the world, we asked, 'What do you look for and admire in a leader (defined as someone whose direction you would willingly follow)?' Then we asked, 'What do you look for and admire in a colleague (defined as someone you'd like to have on your team)?' The number one requirement of a leader—honesty—was also the top-ranking attribute of a good colleague."[24]

RESPONSIBILITY

Responsibility is that element in social or organizational interaction for which a leader will be held personally accountable. As Galindo shared, "When you're truly responsible, you believe that success or failure is up to you, even if you work within a team or are blindsided by unforeseen circumstances. You own your commitment to a result before the fact—before you even take action."[25]

The commitment on which responsibility is based produces ownership and imbues meaning to a task. For leaders, responsibility is many faceted including what is done individually and what is established through the mission and goals of the organization that others carry out.

TRUST

When we think of trust, we think of people who are truthful and dependable. People who, when given a task to undertake (or when given privileged information), can be counted on to give their best to do the task right and see it through to completion. We think of people who will honor the privilege of information (shared with them) that is not for public consumption.

Trust is built on personal accountability and responsibility. And, trust is interactive. It involves two or more people interacting with each other and depending on each other for success. Galindo put it eloquently when she said, "no accountability, no trust."[26]

INTEGRITY

Integrity is the well-spring of trust. It is that flowing current of actions, interactions, and words (communication) done right that builds trust. Integrity is essential to a leader's credibility. According to Bennis, "Integrity simply means moral and intellectual honesty. Without it, we betray ourselves and others and cheapen every endeavor. Integrity is the single quality whose absence we feel most sharply on every level of our national life."[27]

In like fashion, Carly Fiorina stated, "Leadership is about the integrity of one's character."[28] Integrity hinges on what a leader says and does. If a leader's words align with his/her actions and do so in every circumstance, that constancy and unwavering character speaks volumes to those in the organization.

SINCERITY

Like integrity, sincerity is related to trust and via trust to credibility. When there is congruity between a leader's actions and his/her stated objectives, sincerity is established. When the opposite is true, sincerity and credibility diminish. The sense of the leader being sincere in what he/she believes, says, and does is tarnished and his/her sincerity is lost or becomes highly questionable in the eyes of the follower. Not a desirable outcome. However, sincerity like credibility in general can be reestablished or regained but takes a proactive response to the situation that called the leader's sincerity into question.

CREDIBILITY AND LEADERSHIP

So, what is credibility then in terms of its impact on leadership? It is the difference between gaining followers and losing them. It is the difference between being able to assert influence and lacking the influence to affect a situation. It is the difference between having your vision for an organization accepted or rejected. It is the difference between being able to resolve a vital but disputed issue and having the issue left as a festering sore that will negatively impact an organization. It is the difference between being a successful leader and a leader who fails or is derailed.

Credibility is the defining and most significant soft skill characteristic of a leader. It is that element without which being a leader is impossible. Perhaps equally important, it is the essence upon which relationships are built and maintained. Credibility binds together the beliefs, words, and actions of an individual upon which that individual is judged personally and professionally. And, credibility enhances leader acumen (LSA).

Chapter 4

"Recalculating"

Leader Competence

Why is the term "recalculating" utilized when we refer to leader competence? To begin, all leaders need to re-tool or "re-calculate." Doctors don't go to medical school and stop their education. They have to keep on top of the latest information for medicines, medical practice, and referrals. Likewise, biology teachers don't graduate with a bachelor's degree and know all the science they will need to teach over a career. As time moves forward, connections to learned materials and inventions and genetic engineering and the like change the biological implications from the past and for the future.

All professions share the need for practitioners to remain current and to be up-to-date on the latest discoveries, innovations, and techniques for applying those to the tasks of their profession. As leaders, we need to set the example for the organization by working to improve our skillsets as the person in charge.

In the world of the GPS, if the driver varies from the route established, a familiar voice comes from the device with a commanding, "Re-calculating . . . re-calculating." This in effect means that the GPS acknowledges the driver has gone astray and the GPS therefore tries to help the driver back onto the correct course. In an analogous way, if a leader is about to make a misstep, there should be a still, small voice within whispering "recalculating . . . recalculating." This of course is the leader's conscience.

The competent person on a traverse, however, knows when they have purposefully ignored the information given to them via the GPS. Generally, they have done this because they have more or other information available. Of course, most of the time when the driver ignores route guidance, there is a reasonable rationale.

On occasion as one is traveling in the correct direction, there is a need to make a temporary change. Many times, that need takes the form of creature comforts—a restroom break, need to refuel, looking for a place to eat, and sometimes in the form of an emergency. So, the route is changed due to necessity, but not without sacrifice of some sort. In this case the sacrifice is not the route but another variable. Whenever a course is set, any deviation from that course comes at a cost. In this case, the additional expense comes in the form of time. As you are aware, when a destination is entered into a GPS, an ETA is given for the expectation of trip completion. As intended deviations are taken, that ETA moves further and further away.

In the case of competence, once your ETA is established and you share it with others, they will have an expectation regarding your competence. As making adjustments to your route (even when necessary) can impact your arrival time, in the case of a leader, changes may impact your perceived competence.

Developing and maintaining competence in one's chosen field requires not only initial training but continuous renewal. That is, once an aspiring leader has been immersed in the minutiae of his/her field he/she must learn to apply what they have learned. Achieving competence represents a major career accomplishment: being able to function successfully at the highest level within your chosen field.

Competence is more than a one-dimensional concept. It is the amalgamation of critical self-reflection and the perspective of others. For leaders it is not only knowing that you have the requisite knowledge, skills, and ability to get the job done; it is having the respect and trust of those who you work with and who follow you as a leader. It is knowing what to do, how to do it, knowing when and where to act, or having the openness to input and learning that allows those actions. Leaders do not have to have all of the answers all of the time, but they do have to have ability to recognize the potential in any suggested course of action or idea that is proposed. They must be competent and have strong leader acumen (LSA).

In the leader GPS model, a clear separation is made between administrative/managerial "hard" skill competencies such as expertise in financial management, use of technology, scheduling, or facility/grounds management. While these skills have value, being able to build a budget but lacking ability to effectively communicate it to others and/or have others manage the budget once in place limits the effectiveness of having mastered the skill. In like fashion, mastering the use of technology does little good for a leader who cannot utilize that technology to move the people in the organization toward the organization's vision.

As in the case of *credibility*, in this second edition, the authors wanted to ensure *competence* still served as a critical component in the literature as well as in leader followership. The following pages affirm that, indeed, it does.

AN UPDATED REVIEW OF LEADERSHIP COMPETENCE LITERATURE

As noted above, competence is "the amalgamation of critical self-reflection and the perspective of others." Critical self-reflection was discussed in chapter 1. Here, we examine the perspective of others. That perspective has been a central focus of competence research between the first and second editions of this work. While we continue to hold that competence is based on a leader's discernibility, the perception of others and the component parts as described later in this chapter, other researchers are examining different perspectives of competence. For example, Giles in a study "of 195 leaders in 15 countries over 30 global organizations" found that five categories subsume the top ten characteristics associated with competence.[1] According to Giles, those categories can be group into five "themes." Those themes and the percentage of respondents citing them are as follows:

Strong work ethic and safety (67%) = has high ethical and moral standards
Self-organizing (59%) = provides goals and objectives with loose guidelines/ directions
Efficient learning (52%) = has flexibility to change opinions
Nurtures growth (43%) = is committed to my ongoing training
Connection and belonging (56%) = clearly communicates expectations and communicates often and openly.[2]

Summarizing her findings, Giles shared that "Taken together, these attributes are all about creating a safe and trusting environment."[3]

Postuła and Majczyk, in a qualitative study of managers and leaders in sixteen large firms, categorized leader competencies into three categories: knowledge/analytic; skills; and attitude/ability. Those categories include the leader characteristics as follows.

> Knowledge/analytic: combination of technical skills and interpersonal (managerial)—two company owners; interdisciplinarity; identifying problems in the environment; generating solutions to problems
>
> Skills: flexibility; conceptual skills allow to structure the path of development of the organization; comprehensive planning and operational planning; the ability to synthesize the areas of business including knowledge, trends, policies, and further analyze available information; applying data; articulating their beliefs; making valid and sound arguments; convincing people to follow the vision, objectives, goals; forecast, anticipating trends, results; collaboration capabilities; ability to understand and listen to people; supervising work; negotiating skills; ability to establish relationships; managing the direction of business

development, financial management, restructuring employment; entrepreneurial skills—identifying opportunities and exploiting the potential of a business entity; marketing skills; the ability to learn, acquire knowledge

Attitude/ability: respect; sensitivity (engineer-artist); wide view, contact with others, a different point of view; consistency, integrity (fair, ethic); sympathetic; flexible; energetic; thrill-seeking; ambitious; eager to cooperate; independent; courageous; prudent; responsible; honest; determined to obtain success; stubborn[4]

Postuła and Majczyk conclude that "leaders need respect from others even more than managers to reach their goals. In their opinion, it is extremely important for the organisational development from the strategic point of view (for the company, as well as for the leader)."[5]

In a study of leadership for innovation, Portnova and Peiseniece found that "competences that stimulate innovation can be divided into three groups—competences that are equally important for both phases (innovation and implementation, emphasis added) and competences that are more important in each of the phases."[6] The competences as listed by Portnova and Peiseniece are strategical view, implementation strategy, business orientation, result orientation, orientation toward creativity, orientation toward development, team building, and team efficiency. Portnova and Peiseniece go on to list the behaviors characteristic of each competence and the importance of the competence to the invention and implementation phases.

In a different approach, Porvaznik, Ljudvigova, and Čajková cast competence as a separate calculable quotient. They posit that HQ = KQ, AQ, SQ or that "holistic managerial competence (HQ)" is the amalgamation of "knowledge competence (KQ)", "application skill (AQ)" and "social maturity (SQ)."[7] These three variables form the basis of competence and are described as pillars supporting holistic competence.

Knowledge competence is viewed "as the general and professional knowledge is the centre of the first pillar. This pillar is based on the adoption of relevant professional knowledge for the given working position. The second pillar is the application skill, which indicates the standard of practical skills of managerial subjects, which means the ability to take the advantage of the acquired knowledge in everyday use." A third pillar is social maturity and is "based on personal qualities of the employees and managers."[8]

In a somewhat similar approach Heath, Martin, and Shahisaman suggest the concept of global intelligence. As they relate global intelligence (GQ) as "a leadership competency that describes how to be a more successful global leader," and appropriately summarize the common aspects and benefits of emotional intelligence, cultural intelligence, moral intelligence, digital intelligence, and gender intelligence (specifically the importance of self-awareness).[9] A simpler approach is provided by Gupta and Bhal (2017) who share that "Leader competence is dependent on the members' image of his/her leader based on his/her assessments of technical expertise, proficiency and knowledge of the leader."[10]

Maulding Green and Leonard hold that "competence is more than a one-dimensional concept."[11] As Portnova and Peiseniece share "competences do not cover all aspects of personality, but comprise the most important everyday behaviour that enhances the achievement of an organization's strategic goals."[12] The diverse nature of the competence research is intriguing.

Minh, Badir, Quang, and Afsar related competence to leader technical competence (LTC) saying that "LTC (leader technical competence) has a positive relationship with subordinate's learning and innovative work behavior."[13] The importance of technical competence is emphasized by Artz, Goodall, and Oswald who state emphatically that "a boss's technical competence is the single strongest predictor of a worker's job satisfaction."[14] In a study of social and emotional competence and transformational leadership, Wang, Wilhite, and Martino found that "for those school leaders whose self-assessment of their leadership agreed with that of their subordinates, the self-ratings of emotional competence were strongly and significantly correlated with the self-ratings of transformational leadership."[15]

Sturm, Vera, and Crossan introduced the concept of character-competence stating that "merely possessing character and competence is insufficient; rather, they need to be deepened and developed together over time."[16] That development comes about via character-competence entanglement, which "reflects the binding between character and competence, and exists in varying degrees depending on the level of competence, the depth of character, and the strength of the bond between them."[17]

In examining leader competence and warmth, Capozza, Bobbio, Di Bernardo, Falvo, and Pagani "discovered that the perception of one's supervisor as competent, intelligent, capable, and self-assured is linked to key organizational outcomes: lower burnout, more frequent citizenship behaviors and weaker intentions to leave. These competence/outcome connections are mediated by affective organizational commitment."[18] Addressing how women's competence is judged Klatt, Eimler, and Krämer state "regarding competence, women with makeup, pants, or jewelry were rated higher than those wearing the other options, i.e. no makeup, jewelry, or skirt." And, further, they state that "In sum, even subtle changes in styling have a strong impact on how women's leadership abilities are evaluated."[19]

Writing about how to prove yourself after a promotion, Knight suggests that an individual should "project competence."[20] Regardless of the conceptualization of competence and/or the aspect from which it is viewed, competence is a valuable characteristic for a leader. Some even place it as the most important characteristic for a leader. As Gukdo, Dai, Lee, and Kang state,

> a leader's competence in his or her assigned tasks and roles can also be an important influencing factor in determining the quality of the relationship that members form with their leader. A growing body of evidence suggests that the competence of a leader accounts for much of his or her success and remains the most important factor in determining the leader's effectiveness.[21]

As shared by Fransen, Vansteenkiste, Vande Broek, and Boen "competence is one of the three fundamental psychological needs that are essential to foster individuals' intrinsic motivation and engagement."[22] As a leader GPS imperative, the significance of competence cannot be overstated. Competence plays a significant part in how a leader gets things done. It is the "how-to-go-along" with the why of vision and organizational member engagement implicit in the soft skills of emotional intelligence.

True competence in effectively applying these "hard skills" requires mastery of "soft skills/people-centered skills." Based on "soft/people skills" the leader GPS model addresses discernibility, perception, conflict resolution, problem solving, decision-making, planning and implementation, relationship building, and assessment and evaluation skills as composing the core "soft skills" related to competence.

DISCERNIBILITY

A leader, to be effective, must have the skill of discernibility including the ability to discern effective practices from ineffective practices. A leader is discernable when his/her beliefs, thoughts, ideas, words, and actions distinguish him/her from other leaders. The discernible leader is credible in the sense that his/her words and actions are congruent. He/she has displayed the type of ethical behavior, honesty, integrity, and responsibility that establish trust. Of leadership, Bolman and Deal say, "It is not tangible. It exists only in relationships and in the perception of the engaged parties."[23] Their description of leadership fits well with discernibility: it is in the perception and beliefs of peers and followers. And, those perceptions and beliefs are behaviorally based. They are dependent on what a leader does and says.

PERCEPTION

Perception is reality as the old saw goes. What we perceive to be real, for us is real. Perception for a leader is dichotomous. It is how the leader is perceived by others both within and external to an organization. Leader perception is also how the leader perceives individuals within and external to the organization, the functioning of the organization, and the outcomes of organizational processes. How the leader perceives himself/herself is important as well.

We all have a mental image of what an ideal leader should be and would do. And while those images or perceptions of a leader vary as greatly as the number of followers of a leader, there are always commonalities. Gurr and Day,[24] in reporting the characteristics of successful school leaders based on the International Successful School Principalship Project (ISSPP), state, "A major understanding from 12 years of research in the ISSPP is that we can describe what successful school leadership looks like across the world." They found that in summary, successful school leaders:

- have high expectations of all to employ multiple conceptions of leadership (they are not wedded to the use of narrow concepts like instructional or transformational leadership) and utilize a core set of practices focused on setting direction, developing people, leading change and improving teaching and learning;
- model leadership that is both heroic and inclusive;
- foster collaboration and collective endeavor;
- acknowledge and embrace their symbolic role;
- display integrity, trust, and transparency;
- are people centered;
- focus their efforts on the development of others;
- are able to lead in challenging contexts and view challenges as obstacles to overcome rather than problems that are insurmountable;
- develop a range of appropriate personal qualities, with appropriate core values and beliefs articulated and lived (such as a belief that all can learn).

CONFLICT RESOLUTION SKILLS

Conflict is a natural part of being human. Conflict generally begins with disagreement and then, if not resolved, escalates into conflict. Disagreement, of course, can be functional or dysfunctional. When disagreement leads to new thinking or innovative approaches, it is constructive or positive. When disagreement leads to disassociation or outright conflict, the results are most often bad.

Specifically, conflicts (problems) in organizations tend to arise from six sources, disputes, or concerns between or among individuals or groups involving: (1) people (professional interpersonal or group conflicts or in some instances intrapersonal conflicts); (2) tasks to be accomplished; (3) process issues; (4) resource allocation (fiscal, material, human, or informational resources); (5) product or outcome issues; and (6) pressure from internal or external sources.[25]

Unresolved conflicts in any one of these areas can be disruptive. To avoid those bad outcomes a leader must have high-level conflict resolution skills. Bolman and Deal stress reframing conflicts to encourage all sides examine potential satisfactory solutions.[26]

PROBLEM-SOLVING AND DECISION-MAKING SKILLS

Like conflict is a part of human nature, it is the nature of any enterprise that problems will arise. The problems may be small and relatively insignificant or rise to a level that threatens the existence of the organization. No matter where on the spectrum from minor to fatal a problem falls, it is incumbent upon an organizational leader to solve the problem in a timely, positive, and productive manner. The solution must incorporate the best thinking not only of the leader but of organizational members (or, at times, those external to the organization) impacted by the decision.

Both the reframing suggested by Bolman and Dean and Covey's win-win process are applicable problem-solving paradigms. A leader must determine who should be involved in the decision-making process, proactively seek their input, and based upon available information arrive at the best decision. Of course, in some instances the leader will have, perforce, to make unilateral decisions.

RELATIONSHIP BUILDING

In discussing credibility, we shared that credibility is the essence upon which relationships are built and maintained. That straightforward statement captures the vital importance of relationships to leader success. Leadership is a social process. That process plays out within an organization and as a part of the interface between an organization and individuals and entities external to the organization. Without the ability to build and maintain working relationships, a leader is doomed to failure: as the poet John Donne said, "no man is an island unto himself."

A leader must work in cooperation and coordination with others to achieve organizational success and through organizational success, success for himself/herself and members of the organization. Reina and Reina[27] say, "It is people working in relationship with one another that ultimately delivers results."

PLANNING AND IMPLEMENTATION SKILLS

In a later chapter we will discuss leadership vision but we mention it here as an introduction to planning and implementation. Suffice it to say here that vision without planning and implementation skills is a hollow vessel. Skills in planning and implementation allow a leader to facilitate his/her vision for the organization. Chief among planning and implementation skills is the ability to bring together and motivate individuals and groups.

ASSESSMENT AND EVALUATION

A leader must also be able to assess and evaluate the intricacies of the social and political interactions within the organization and, at times, the interaction of organization members with individuals or entities external to the organization. And, a leader must be able to assess and evaluate the task processes that lead to the desired outcomes of the organization. A leader must also be critically reflective of his/her actions. Without that reflection, mistakes will be repeated and opportunities will be missed.

COMPETENCE AND LEADERSHIP

Competence is to credibility as the keystone is to a masonry arch. With a solid keystone the arch holds solidly and will fail only if the surrounding structure is damaged or the strength of the structure eroded over time. Competence is the keystone that allows a leader to bind (and over time) hold the organization together by not only properly carrying out the hard skills tasks of his/her job but by also successfully applying the essential soft skills concomitant with the hard skill tasks. Only when organizational members believe a leader is competent can the leader truly be said to have credibility. A leader with high LSA has a greater probability of establishing through his/her actions that he/she is competent and therefore enhances his/her credibility.

Chapter 5

Lost Satellite Reception: Leader Inspiration

Occasionally when traveling, you get to an area that is completely unrecognized by your GPS. Or perhaps it's a very cloudy day and your GPS cannot receive signals to give you directions. Or something more exotic may be happening. "Space weather" can occur when there is a strong solar storm or someone may be using an illegal jamming device or interference from a close by adjacent band transmitter may be occurring.[1]

As GPS devices are used, data is gathered, which helps them acquire satellites quickly at the start of each use. If a device is used daily, it should be able to acquire satellites in a minute or less. Using a GPS device while it is outdoors with a clear view of the entire sky is the ideal condition for acquiring satellites.

At the time when it is not working so quickly, perhaps a little inspiration is needed. It could be that this is the first time the system has been asked to perform in a while. It would be completely understandable for it to take a wee bit longer for it to get the inspiration to start humming. Conceivably, it might not be responsive to directions if it is improperly positioned or has been inactive for a while. Many of us need a warm cup of coffee to inspire us to move forward in the mornings.

Sometimes when new maps are loaded (or the GPS has had a master reset), it is slower to respond. Similarly changes to policy, procedures, and protocol make the leader a little less certain when making decisions. On occasion the leader must take a few minutes to think through the new directives to be certain they are conforming to new standards. Similarly, and almost without exception, beginning a new route requires inspiration. Sometimes the inspiration that is needed is small, other times a bit larger. But the time invested in "inspiration" can reap huge benefits.

The LSA concept identifies inspirational leaders as those who galvanize an organization to action, leading to individual and organizational success. Many times, inspirational leaders are charismatic. However, charisma is not a prerequisite for the inspirational leader. As Baldoni stated, "Charisma enhances one's presence but it is not essential."[2] Peter Drucker, in discussing effective executives and charisma, shared that, "Harry Truman did not have one ounce of charisma . . . yet he was among the most effective chief executives in U.S. history."[3] In this same vein, Baldoni[4] related, "While inspirational leaders are often charismatic, as were John Kennedy and Ronald Reagan, leadership inspiration comes more from the power of possibilities. Bill Gates is an exemplar. Gates does not warm to the spotlight the way celebrities do. It is the power of his ideas, first at Microsoft and now at the Bill and Melinda Gates Foundation. *His inspiration* draws bright capable people to him the way moths are drawn to flames."

Another moving leader, Martin Luther King, Jr., is one of the first names that comes to mind when we think of being inspired.[5] Although King's lifetime mission was to improve the quality of life, as well as justice for his contemporaries, he did not always intend to do it via means of the pulpit. Initially, King believed the best way to exact change would be as an advocate of peace through the justice system as an attorney.

Having been reared in the church, he mused over that platform being used as a vehicle for nonviolent inspiration of the civil rights movement. Over time, he determined that it could, and inspire he did. The final years of his highly charismatic and short life were spent inspiring those around him to reach for a more equal and just society.

In reality the majority of leaders are not charismatic but attempt to inspire individuals within the organization through words and deeds. They attempt to put the individuals who make up the organization (and through them the organization itself) in the best position to succeed. At the height of the recent economic downturn, a time when leadership was often in question Baldoni[6] held that,

> Needed in this downturn are men and women who can inspire, not simply with the power of their personality but with the power of their imagination. Such vision need not be reserved solely for those at the top of the pyramid; rather it can be recognized and nurtured by those who are in position to groom and promote the next generation of leaders. Here are three attributes to look for.
>
> **Realism.** Inspirational leaders are rooted in reality. They know the facts but remain undeterred. This sense separates them from fools who are quick to rush into things before considering consequences. Inspirational leaders are keenly aware of what could go wrong and are honest about it. It is this honesty that draws capable contributors. They sense the leader knows the facts but is willing to experiment as well as persevere.

Improvement. Wanting to make things better is essential to inspiration. Therefore, inspirational leaders value innovations. They are inherently creative because they are not satisfied with the status quo. Very importantly they seek to open doors for people who can innovate in their function, be it product development or logistics. They encourage employees to think for themselves.

Optimism. You must believe in the better tomorrow. This is easy to do when the economy is rising but more difficult when it is shrinking. Optimism for the inspirational leader is not merely inherent; it is contagious. Others feel it and want to feed off it. This is essential to getting the work done now and developing next generation initiatives that will position the organization for success over the long term.

Wilson and Rice,[7] addressing inspirational leadership "in times of adversity," share that

> Inspirational leadership can breathe the capacity for responding to adversity into the heart and soul of an organization, and this capacity becomes part of the organization's culture. If people are involved in building and accomplishing the inspirational leader's vision for the organization, if their work is connected to that vision and to their own motivations and values, the value of the resulting commitment to the overall success of the organization cannot be overstated. If the organization's culture is one that inspires rather than oppresses, it can only have the effect of creating a more productive organization and profitable bottom line.

From a North American perspective, inspirational leadership blends the *charismatic, transformational,* and *value-based* styles of leading.

- Charismatic leaders bring unique gifts to their organization. They are visionary and have a highly developed sense of strategic timing. They are unconventional and willing to take calculated risks.
- Transformational leaders develop special relationships with their followers. They challenge the status quo and pay attention to their followers' desires to find meaning in work and for personal development.
- Value-based leaders make the daily work of their followers more meaningful. They help their organizations develop an appealing vision of what lies in the future and generate confidence that the vision can be achieved.

But difficult times are not the sole realm for the emergence or need for inspirational leaders. Inspirational leaders are needed in good times as much as bad times and in fact may act like a deterrent from hardship. In *Catalyzing Inspirational Leadership: Approaches and Metrics for Twenty-First-Century Executives*, Seidman[8] offers these suggestions for leaders willing to take the "journey to inspirational leadership" to improve performance for individuals and organization.

Rethink fundamentals. Everybody knows changing culture is important, but we tend to approach it in an ad hoc fashion. Authentically understanding, shaping, and leveraging your culture will differentiate your organization in the marketplace and drive sustainable growth and impact.
Focus on a higher purpose. Purpose is enduring. It connects your actions to significance. Purpose makes businesses sustainable.
Give trust away. Trust begets trust. Employees who feel truly trusted are less likely to betray that trust because they understand innately that it works to their benefit.
Scale values and get deliberate with culture. Many companies are deeply stuck. They understand instinctively that the financial and environmental crises of our time require new behaviors. They're just beginning to take the journey. But to be activated, individuals must personally commit to changing how they think, how they decide, and how they behave.
Embrace transparency. There are no more secrets. This is a twenty-first-century reality. If your actions don't match your words, your reputation and bottom line will suffer.[8]

These same practices and ideas hold true for the inspirational leader's interaction with individuals and entities external to the organization. They inspire belief and faith in the organization, its goals and purposes, and move those external individuals and entities to support the individuals within the organization and through them the organization itself.

These leaders encourage individuals to grow professionally and personally and provide the resources to promote that growth process. They are passionate, enthusiastic about what they do. They come across as genuine. They are unrelenting optimists and bring seemingly boundless energy to what they do. Simply put, they inspire by being themselves.

INSPIRING SUCCESS: A FRESH LOOK

Once again, as the authors revisit the leader GPS imperatives, taking a renewed look at the impact of inspiration on followers was needed. The following pages, revealing the most current literature on inspiration, renew and affirm its necessity in the toolbox of the grounded and forward-thinking leader.

A quote from Garton and Mankins sets the stage for a fresh look at a leader's ability to inspire. Garton and Mankins share that

> Most of us know how important inspiration can be in everyday life. In the workplace, as one pundit put it, employees react differently when they encounter a wall. Satisfied employees hold a meeting to discuss what to do about walls. Engaged employees begin looking around for ladders to scale the wall. Inspired employees break right through it.[9]

That quote speaks to the power of inspiration. But, is it well to keep in mind Garton and Mankins's expansion of that statement when they say that "to be sure, it's probably unrealistic to think that you can inspire every employee in your organization—each individual works for different reasons. But many people do seek fulfillment in their jobs. If you aren't trying to inspire these employees, you are leaving real money on the table."[10] We would argue that a leader should be trying to inspire all members of his/her organization. Whether attempting to inspire the few or the many, it is best to remember Dembowski's admonition regarding inspiration "people don't often need, or respond well to, being managed. They are best led to higher performance."[11] Inferred is that inspiration, like almost all aspects of leadership, requires subtlety.

As Myers shared, "Grand announcements and dictates rarely prove to be effective in the modern workplace. Instead, successful leadership is all about subtlety." Subtlety can be very powerful. Bligh and Hess, reflecting on their study of Alan Greenspan, the longtime Chairman of Federal Reserve, noted that "Greenspan's success as a leader may lie in his ability to subtly impact or marginally shift his followers' responses."[12]

A leader who starts out saying "I am here to inspire you" may very well have the opposite effect. In a series of studies of leader charisma (often associated with inspirational leadership) and leader effectiveness, involving 800 business leaders globally and around 7,500 of their superiors, peers, and subordinates, Vergauwe, Wille, Hofmans, Kaiser, and De Fruyt found that "while having at least a moderate level of charisma is important, having too much may hinder a leader's effectiveness."[13] This is an example of the "too-much-of-a good-thing" effect (discussed more fully in chapter 9). The key is to be humble and let your words and actions speak to the type of leader you are.

Good bosses, according to Maner, switch between two fundamentally different leadership styles, "dominance and prestige." Contrasting dominance and prestige Maner says,

> Prestige, in contrast, means influencing others by displaying signs of wisdom and expertise and being a role model. Prestige allows people to influence others even in the absence of formal authority or power. Prestigious leaders enjoy being respected and admired, but they aren't as interested as dominant leaders are in having power or always getting their way. Indeed, prestige-oriented leaders often allow others to set the course, while *subtly* (emphasis added) directing people from behind.[14]

That subtle direction is the result of exercising influence in interpersonal interaction. Morgan describes four components of influence: positional power, emotion, expertise, and mastery of the dance of human interaction. Of that final aspect Morgan says

The final aspect of influence is the *subtlest* (emphasis added) of the four, and as such rarely can trump either positional authority or passion. But in rare instances, artfully manipulated, I have seen it prevail. What is it? It is the mastery of the dance of human interaction. We have very little conscious awareness of this aspect of influence, but we are all participants in it with more or less expertise. We learn at a very early age that conversation is a pas de deux, a game that two (or more) people play that involves breathing, winking, nodding, eye contact, head tilts, hand gestures, and a whole series of subtle non-verbal signals that help both parties communicate with one another.[15]

The axiom for leadership seems to be that a leader should be eclectic in his/her exercise of leadership, moving from one style to the other as the situation dictates. This position is consistent with the long-standing fundamental understanding of good leadership and applies equally to inspirational leadership. One approach does not fit/work for all or in all circumstances.

Recent research on a leader's ability to inspire has been with focus on various approaches to inspiring others in the workplace. Seppala shares that an organization as an entity can be inspirational to its members by insuring that the work undertaken as meaning, "No matter what your organization does—whether it's offering a service or building products—it is important that your culture be infused with meaning."[16] Leaders too, according to Seppala, can be sources of inspiration "when they act selflessly, proving they care more about the group than themselves."[17]

It is the tales or stories told about leaders by others that hold great potential for inspiring others, especially if the leader is seldom on site. According to Washburn and Galvin, "stories told informally by what we call leader surrogates—individuals who have developed admiration and respect for you and actively share favorable information about you, whether personal or secondhand—are more powerful in helping you to inspire your people than the formal communications you crank out."[18]

And how do those surrogates develop admiration and respect for the leader? "Leaders who demonstrate that they live by their own standards inspire surrogates."[19] Gallo supports both Seppala and Washburn and Galvin when he shares that "inspiring leaders ignite passion and loyalty by infusing their brand with a higher mission—and they do it through story. They wrap their product, service, company, or cause in a narrative that speaks to the core of what makes us human—a search for meaning."[20]

For Seidman and Leaf, the key to inspiring other is moral authority. "Moral leaders inspire and elevate others. Those with moral authority understand what they can demand of others and what they must inspire in them. Honesty, for example, can be demanded. But loyalty must be inspired."[21] Moral authority is a steadfast measure of ability to inspire. But, what must a leader do to inspire others and what does it mean to be inspired?

Again, inspirational leaders take different paths to the same goal. Some leaders inspire; others, by doing what seems essential, according to Zenger and Folkman.[22] Other leaders, shares Tasler, inspire by creating a circumstance that allows individuals to "bring some new idea to life after becoming spontaneously aware of new possibilities."[23] For Fransen, Vande Broek, Boen, Steffens, Haslam, and Vanbeselaere the effect of inspirational leadership is to build confidence.[24]

Whatever the leader does to inspire others, the results are uplifting. Hedges, based on the work of Thrash and Elliot, holds that "three elements that occur when we're inspired: we see new possibilities, we're receptive to an outside influence, and we feel energized and motivated."[25] Inspirational leaders, Hoffner shares, "not only allow individuals to be innovative and take greater ownership in their work and projects, but they also encourage them to do so. Ultimately, we feel trust, loyalty and respect for these types of leaders because we, in turn, feel trust, loyalty and respect from them."[26] Heller, Notgrass, and Conner see inspiration as resulting from the "level of extra effort" given by organizational members.[27]

Beck shares that "When people are inspired, they aspire to reach new heights/goals and resolve to overcome obstacles, challenges, and fears. They begin to dream bigger and regain hope that they can achieve those dreams."[28] And Garton says, "When employees aren't just engaged, but inspired, that's when organizations see real breakthroughs."[29] And yet, perhaps the best summary is shared by Bird who states that

> Inspiration takes place in a unique way for each of us as individuals when three elements come together in a magical combination:
> The triggers we encounter in the external world—the situations, events and people we experience as we progress through our lives.
> The mindsets we bring to interpret these experiences and relate them to our own selves.
> The motivations we feel internally, especially the values, interests and talents we have most passion for.[30]

Magical or not, inspiration is something (consciously or unconsciously) that we all seek. As viewed in LSA, a leader's ability to inspire is essential to success. It is also what moves people to strive for success. The following subsections have been identified by the authors as essential component parts of the fore-described GPS skillset imperative, inspiration.

ENTHUSIASTIC

Like many of the characteristics related to the Leadership GPS skillset, being enthusiastic has a dual nature. For a leader to be enthusiastic he/she must have, display, and communicate enthusiasm individually toward the work of his/her organization including his/her role in the organization. He/she must be well grounded and have a firm grasp of their individual beliefs.

A leader must also be capable of generating enthusiasm in organizational members. In their discussion of inspirational leaders, Zenger and Folkman[31] list one type as *"Enthusiasts."* They show passion, vitality, and vigor. Passive behaviors evade them and dynamic decisions are naturally made. They are extraverts who generate energy and excitement. Enthusiasts breathe life into organizations. The companion behavior is *making an emotional connection.*

ENERGETIC

One could say that energy or being energetic is the catalyst that ignites enthusiasm. Imagine doing anything that you enjoy tremendously including work and then try to imagine that doing the same thing with no emotion or energy. The scenario takes a decidedly sad turn. Those sad outcomes can be avoided if leaders apply their energy wisely. Their energy must be utilized to drive fulfilling the mission of the organization. And, they must be mindful that while energy is renewable it is not infinite. As with enthusiasm, energy needs to be focused, directed, and applied in such a fashion as to engage peers and followers. A leader must be energetic and should generate energy in others. Patterson and Kelleher wrote, "Energy is essential to effective leadership."[32]

PASSIONATE

Leaders who believe in what they are doing are passionate. Passion for what you do arises from the desire to do what you undertake well, to pursue perfection and success at the highest levels. Passion is the sustaining element that allows the inspirational leader to have an ongoing thirst for success and to inspire passion for the organization's work within organizational members. Without passion, energy is soon expended and enthusiasm dwindles. Love holds that "As a leader, it's not sufficient to merely understand the passions that drive you or your staff. You must also master the application of passion-driven strengths and carefully manage the vulnerabilities to which someone with your passions might succumb."[33]

OPTIMISTIC

Optimism is yet another dimension of inspiration that tends to drive success. Optimism is based on the belief that actions and outcomes will have positive effect and impact. No difficult situation is impossible to rectify. If, as a leader, you are not optimistic, it is difficult, if not impossible, to convince others of the realistic worth of a decision or action or the shared purpose articulated in the mission and vision statement of a business or school. It is in remaining realistic that leaders are best able to utilize their optimism.

GENUINE

Genuineness is the most significant consideration in relation to inspirational leadership. Enthusiasm, energy, passion, optimism, and courage play vital roles. They fire the esprit de corps and light the way for success. But, unless a leader is clearly perceived as being genuine, having a genuine interest in the success of the individuals that make up an organization, and vested in the success of the organization itself, as opposed to simply seeking to serve his/her own best interests and that path to success, it is unlikely that he/she will be seen as genuine. As MacFarlane[34] said so eloquently, "Genuine (authentic) leadership impresses and inspires, and this is the heart of true leadership that influences successful and sustained positive changes in individuals, groups, and organizations."

COURAGEOUS

In all organizations there will be times when courage is needed to face difficult and trying situations and times. Inspirational leaders have the courage to face dilemmas head on when strengthened by their belief in themselves and the organization. They call upon their inner compass to guide them to the proper decisions and actions. They are unafraid to admit errors and to take proper corrective action if that is what is called for. They are courageous.

But where does that courage come from? Returning to the theme from our discussion of competence, courage is also about doing "what is right." It is not choosing the safe path or the path of least resistance. It is the fortitude to hold yourself accountable for all that you say and do.

INSPIRATION AND LEADERSHIP

Inspirational leadership in the LSA/GPS model leads to success by building upon the bulwark of credibility and competence. Those with high LSA inspire based on the value they place on the work and the people they work with. They also realize that inspiration is one of those elements of leadership that is best handled and produced with subtlety. That is while some actions, activities, and utterances of a leader will clearly be designed to inspire; true inspiration for both the leader and peers and followers comes from within by finding value and meaning in the work they do. The most successful leaders are those that inspire by being true to themselves and to the purpose of their organization.

Chapter 6
"Arriving at Your Destination"
Leader Vision

When planning a trip, you generally start with your final destination in mind. So, for fun, let's imagine we are going on a trip to Disney World to ride the rides and see Mickey and Minnie. Or perhaps you'd prefer an imaginary trip to the Grand Canyon or Niagara Falls to see nature's awesome display, or even to Anchorage, Alaska, as a departure point for an Alaskan Cruise. No matter the destination, once you know where you want to go, and the address of the location you will be traveling to, the GPS can help you to arrive safely and in a timely fashion.

If you don't have a destination in mind, or if you don't have a plan for your vacation time, you might just decide to spend it all at home. In order for a GPS to work effectively, you must have a vision about where you are heading. Once you have made that decision, the GPS will happily provide you with assistance about the best and quickest routes to get there.

The point is that the GPS *is only a tool* to take you to where *you choose* to go. You have to know where you want to go and program the GPS accordingly using the best detailed information you have or can obtain. Then you must trust the GPS to get you there. In like fashion, a leader must know where he/she wants to take the organization. A leader must have a vision of the ultimate destination and the path, including any side trips or stops along the way, in order to reach that destination. He/she must have or obtain the best detailed information that can be utilized to develop that vision and to carry it to fruition.

In the leader GPS model, as in consideration of leadership in general, vison is a vital component of leadership success. Burt Nanus,[1] a respected leader in vision research, shared that,

> A *vision* is a realistic, credible, attractive future for an organization. It is a carefully formulated statement of intentions that defines a destination or future state

of affairs that an individual or group finds particularly desirable. The right *vision* is an idea so powerful that it literally jump starts the future by calling forth the energies, talents, and resources to make things happen. A visionary leader is one who has the ability to formulate a compelling *vision* for the future of his or her organization, gain commitment to it, and translate that *vision* into reality by making the necessary organizational changes.

From a somewhat different perspective, Collins and Porras say of vision, "A well-conceived vision consists of two major components: core ideology and envisioned future."[2] They describe these two components:

> Core ideology defines the enduring character of an organization—a consistent identity that transcends product or market life cycles, technological breakthroughs, management fads, and individual leaders. In fact, the most lasting and significant contribution of those who build visionary companies is the core ideology.
>
> The second primary component of the vision framework is envisioned future. It consists of two parts: a 10-to-30-year audacious goals plus vivid descriptions of what it will be like to achieve the goal. We recognize that the phrase envisioned future is somewhat paradoxical. On the one hand, it conveys concreteness—something visible, vivid, and real. On the other hand, it involves a time yet unrealized—with its dreams, hopes, and aspirations.[3]

Bennis,[4] in addressing 21st century leadership, said that "Given the nature and constancy of change and the transnational challenges facing American business leadership, the key to making the right choices will come from understanding and embodying the leadership qualities necessary to succeed in the volatile and mercurial global economy." Of those qualities he shared that "While leaders come in every size, shape, and disposition—short, tall, neat, sloppy, young, old, male, and female—there is at least one ingredient that every leader I talked with shared: a concern with a guiding purpose, an overarching vision."[5]

Further Bennis shared[6] that "Leaders have a clear idea of what they want to do—personally and professionally—and the strength to persist in the face of setbacks, even failures. They know where they are going, and why . . . I think of it this way: *Leaders manage the dream*. All leaders have the capacity to create a compelling vision, one that takes people to a new place, and then to translate that vision into reality." Kouzes and Posner report[7] based on their research that

> The number one requirement of a leader—honesty—was also the top-ranking attribute of a good colleague. But the second-highest requirement of a leader, that he or she be forward-looking, applied only to the leader role. Just 27% of respondents selected it as something they want in a colleague, whereas 72%

wanted it in a leader. (Among respondents holding more-senior roles in organizations, the percentage was even greater, at 88%.) No other quality showed such a dramatic difference between leader and colleague.

Kotter, in regard to leaders and vision[8] stated, "Leaders gather a broad range of data and look for patterns, relationships, and linkages that help explain things. What's more, the direction-setting aspect of leadership does not produce plans; it creates vision and strategies. In further explanation, Kotter shared that

> Most discussions of vision have a tendency to degenerate into the mystical. The implication is that a vision is something mysterious that mere mortals, even talented ones, could never hope to have. But developing good business direction isn't magic. It is a tough, sometimes exhausting process of gathering and analyzing information. People who articulate such visions aren't magicians but broad-based strategic thinkers who are willing to take risks.
>
> Nor do visions and strategies have to be brilliantly innovative; in fact, some of the best are not. Effective business visions regularly have an almost mundane quality, usually consisting of ideas that are already well known. The particular combination or patterning of the ideas may be new, but sometimes even that is not the case.[9]

Similarly, in outlining the critical steps to successfully leading change, Kotter shared that one of the primary steps is "Creating a vision to help direct the change effort. Developing strategies for achieving that vision."[10]

In discussion of organizational success and the importance of promoting employee engagement, Goleman[11] said, "If a leader is to articulate such shared values effectively, he or she must first look within to find a genuinely heartfelt guiding vision." He held as well that "truly great, leaders need to expand their focus to a farther horizon line, even beyond decades, while taking their systems understanding to a much finer focus. And their leadership needs to reshape systems themselves."[12]

Stephen Covey listed vision[13] as the first of four attributes of great leaders. Of vision, he said,

> *Vision.* Seeing a future state with the mind's eye is vision. It's applied imagination. All things are created twice: first, a mental creation; second, a physical creation. Vision starts the process of reinvention. It represents desire, dreams, hopes, goals, and plans. These dreams are not just fantasies—they are reality without physicality, like a construction blueprint. Most of us don't envision or realize our potential, even though we all have the power, energy, and capacity to reinvent our lives. Memory is past. It is finite. Vision is future. It is infinite. The most important vision is having a sense of self, a sense of your own destiny, mission, role, purpose and meaning. When testing your own personal vision,

first ask: Does the vision tap into my voice, energy, and talent? Does it give me a sense of "calling," a cause worthy of my commitment? Acquiring such meaning requires profound personal reflection to transcend our autobiography, rise above our memory, and create a magnanimity of spirit toward others. We need to consider not only the vision of what's possible "out there" but also the vision of what we see in other people, their unseen potential. Vision is about more than just getting things done; it is about discovering and expanding our view of others, affirming them, believing in them, and helping them discover their voice and realize their potential. Seeing people through the lens of their potential and their best actions, rather than through the lens of their current behavior or weaknesses, generates positive energy.

Engaging others in the development and realization of the guiding vision for an organization is as important as the organizational vision of the leader. Organizations succeed not only on the work of the leader but more so on the work of the organizational members. Kouzes and Posner[14] set forth the following steps to create a shared vision:

> As counterintuitive as it might seem, then, the best way to lead people into the future is to connect with them deeply in the present. The only visions that take hold are shared visions—and you will create them only when you listen very, very closely to others, appreciate their hopes, and attend to their needs. The best leaders are able to bring their people into the future because they engage in the oldest form of research: They observe the human condition.

Expanding on the requirements to create a shared vision, Kouzes and Posner state,

> So how do new leaders develop this forward-looking capacity? First, of course, they must resolve to carve out time from urgent but endless operational matters. But even more important, as leaders spend more time looking ahead, they must not put too much stock in their own prescience. This point needs to be underscored because, somehow, through all the talk over the years about the importance of vision, many leaders have reached the unfortunate conclusion that they as individuals must be visionaries. With leadership development experts urging them along, they've taken to posing as emissaries from the future, delivering the news of how their markets and organizations will be transformed.
>
> Bad idea! This is not what constituents want. Yes, leaders must ask, "What's new? What's next? What's better?"—but they can't present answers that are only theirs. Constituents want visions of the future that reflect their own aspirations. They want to hear how their dreams will come true and their hopes will be fulfilled. We draw this conclusion from our most recent analysis of nearly one million responses to our leadership assessment, "The Leadership Practices Inventory." The data tell us that what leaders struggle with most is

communicating an image of the future that draws others in—that speaks to what others see and feel.[15]

Nanus[16] said of gaining commitment of organizational members, "the key to gaining widespread commitment to a new vision, therefore, is to present the vision in such a way that people will want to participate and will freely choose to do so." While the above examples spring from the business world, the same emphasis of vision is seen in the public sector. From a meta-analysis spanning the years 1995–2012, Murphy and Torre[17] conclude that "Vision is a hallmark variable in the school improvement algorithm. Second, leadership is the keystone element in developing, implementing, and shepherding the school's vision."

Méndez-Morse,[18] writing for the Southwest Educational Development Laboratory, stated that,

> Visionary educational leaders have a clear picture of what they want to accomplish. The vision of their school or district provides purpose, meaning, and significance to the work of the school and enables them to motivate and empower the staff to contribute to the realization of the vision ... In addition to providing a picture of the future, a vision inspires people to work to make it come true. It motivates people to join the campaign to realize the desired vision.

She goes onto to share four steps[19] to developing a shared vision. According to Méndez-Morse, these four steps facilitate a collaborative development of a shared vision and written vision statement. Briefly these steps are:

1. Know your organization—clarify the nature and purpose
2. Involve critical individuals—include those affected
3. Explore the possibilities—consider possible futures
4. Put it in writing—vision is committed to paper[20]

The following pages affirm our initial thoughts regarding the importance of vision for the leader. Furthermore, this collection of work regarding the leader and vision is the most worthy and current in the literature at the time of this research.

ENVISIONING SUCCESS: A FRESH LOOK

Describing the importance of leader vision in the prior edition, we shared that "Vision opens the door for the credible, competent, inspirational leader to opportunities for success."[21] Implicit in that statement was the understanding that vision is central to reaching *next level success* as a leader. Vision is the key that unlocks the door to *next level leadership*. Reflecting this same line of thought, Ashkenas and Manville describe six fundamental skills that every leader should have or display to get to the next level whether as an aspiring or experienced leader.

At the top of that list is vision about which Ashkenas and Manville say that leaders should

> Shape a vision that is exciting and challenging for your team (or division/unit/organization). Translate that vision into a clear strategy about what actions to take, and what not to do. Recruit, develop, and reward a team of great people to carry out the strategy.[22]

Quinn and Thakor (2018) take vision one step farther when they hold that to create a purpose driven organization a leader must "envision an inspired workforce."[23] To do so, Quinn and Thakor urge leaders to seek out "excellence, examine the purpose that drives the excellence, and then imagine it imbuing your entire workforce."[24]

The value of human capital represented in having an organizational vision embracing the idea of acting to produce a work force dedicated to accomplishing the goals of the organizations is inestimable. The argument that leader vision is vital is further bolstered by current research since the publication of the first edition of this work.

Research dealing with vision has encompassed a spectrum of possibilities for creating and communicating a shared organizational vision to generate organizational success. Baur, J. Ellen, Buckley, Ferris, Allison, McKenny, and Short, in a study of how leaders articulate their vision, stated, "our analysis showed that a (leader) profile that included a more balanced usage of charismatic rhetoric dimensions was more effective for influencing followers."[25]

In a similar study, Smith supports the finding of Baur et al. stating that "a leader's communication of organizational vision may influence the development of passion."[26] Jensen, Moynihan, and Salomonsen, in a study of communicating vision in transformational leadership settings, observe that "findings suggest that any consideration of the transformational leadership toolkit is incomplete without parallel attention to the communication behaviors crucial for getting the vision through to the employees."[27]

In a study of the moderating effect of shrewd vision, Strese, Keller, Flatten, and Brettel share that "CEOs who are passionate about inventing play a significant role with regard to radical innovation and that the degree to which a firm's members share its vision is positively correlated with this relationship."[28] Passion for work, as we have said, is necessary for leader success. Ndalamba, Caldwell, and Anderson rightly contend that leadership vision "includes the ability to not only discern one's own best self but to see the greatness in others."[29]

For a leader to succeed his/her followers must succeed; it is in the joining of a leader and followers in mutually setting and pursuing a vision that bring success and potentially greatness. Decker and Decker share four maxims for creating leader vision

> Think about your audience—What do they care about most?
> Target the message to their needs—How is the vision relevant to them?
> Lay out action steps—What are specific measurable goals and deadlines?
> Engage their emotions—How will they benefit in the end?[30]

A similar admonition is found by Seijts and Gandz who note that "a key requirement of any vision is that it reflect a purpose that inspires employees on a personal level."[31] In a study of launching and leading intense teams, Webber and Webber identified "that team members are more committed to the team and will provide extra effort when the vision of the team's work is clear and the goals and objectives have been defined."[32]

Peterson adds in complementary fashion that leaders should "motivate others, have a clear idea of where to take their group, and the ability to communicate a vision that resonates."[33] As shared by Bonau, "articulating an exciting and inspirational vision, which communicates the common goal in a meaningful and emotional way, is a central aspect of being inspirational as a leader."[34] Reflecting the same idea, Chai, Hwang, and Joo share that "when team members understand and consider that the organizations' mission, vision, and values are appropriate, they are more likely to align their values and goals with those of the organization."[35]

Kirkpatrick summarizes the significance of effectively communicating the organizational vision based on her study of the human performance technology (HPT) model when she says,

> All of the leaders I interviewed agreed on the importance of communicating the vision statement repeatedly to employees so that all elements of the company were aligned with the vision. Communicating the vision statement entailed much more than sending a single email or printing posters with the statement. The leaders communicated their vision in many different ways and integrated its communication into their daily conversations.[36]

Mumford, Todd, Higgs, and McIntosh in a study of cognitive skills and leadership performance identified nine key skills leaders need. Prominent among those skills was sensemaking/visioning. They further state that

> Wisdom, of course, is of some importance to leader problem-solving performance, in fact, because wisdom may help leaders craft visions appropriate for followers. The term "craft visions" here is of some importance because it implies leaders must think about followers, their values and identity, in communicating

plans, adjusting plans, and the vision being articulated to maximize their impact on followers.[37]

Sensemaking and visioning are conjoined practices that reinforce a leader's shared vision. Karl Weick is generally credited with introducing the concept of sensemaking, which he describes as involving "the ongoing retrospective development of plausible images that rationalize what people are doing."[38] Or as Brewer said in simpler terms, sensemaking is "the process of creating a shared understanding."[39]

It is easy to see that vison or visioning is closely related to sensemaking as vision defines what an individual or group is *making sense of*. The relationship between sensemaking and vision (visioning) concepts is clearly defined by Watts, Steele, and Mumford in the following remark: "Sensemaking, and the underlying cognitive mechanisms that support this critical leader capacity, can be developed as a leadership skill—a skill that supports the formation and articulation of viable leader visions."[40]

Maximizing the impact of organizational vision can be seen in the results of studies of vision. In a 2016 study on the effect of vision and role clarity on team performance, Lynn and Kalay found that "vision clarity has a positive effect on team performance."[41] Mombourquette, in a study of successful school principals, found that principals from all school levels who led high-performing schools had a clear vision for the school, communicated that vision widely, involved others in the development and refinement of that vision, and used data to support their efforts to drive the school improvement efforts.[42]

Ashford, Wellman, Sully De Luque, De Stobbeleir, and Wollan, in a study of leader feedback and vision articulation in a sample of CEOs and top management teams (TMTs), found that "members from 65 firms, both CEO feedback seeking and vision articulation exhibited positive direct relationships with firm performance."[43]

Viewed from any perspective, leader vision is a critical element in organizational success. Zemme, Cuddihy, and Carey share that "every leader understands the importance of the first hundred days or the first year in office—the period during which one must assess and diagnose, formulate a vision and a strategy, and create the early wins that build trust and legitimacy."[44] But, vision must also be maintained and renewed periodically. One way to establish and sustain long-term vison is to be adaptive and flexible and to create an organizational culture of excellence.

Of adaptability, in the companion book, Growing Your Leadership: Scenarios from Practicing K12 Prinicpals,[45, 46] we reference Bennis and Thomas who stated that "to the extent that any single quality determines success, that quality is adaptive capacity."[47] Paul, in discussing creating a culture of excellence, shares that flexibility is a critical factor, one of pillars that support excellence, and that flexibility "helps us respond to unique situations whenever and wherever they occur."[48]

Regarding a culture of excellence, Paul shares that in "a culture of excellence, everyone enjoys what they are doing, has a clear understanding of how important their work is, and makes decisions based on the company's mission, vision, and values."[49] Finally, culture is *enduring*. As Groysberg, Lee, Price, and Cheng share culture "can direct the thoughts and actions of group members over the long term."[50] LSA can enable a leader to create, develop, implement, and sustain a shared organizational vision over time and open the gateway to *next level leadership*.

Vision, as defined in the leader GPS model, is the end result of a process whereby a leader develops objectives or goals and sets a direction for an organization based on the shared input of all stakeholders. Defining vision is simple. Creating a shared vision and, more significantly, effectively communicating that shared vision, and transforming it into action is the challenge. The components discussed in the remainder of this chapter, commitment, sense of direction, professionalism, decisiveness, work ethic, and concern for the future form the basis of leadership vision in the leader GPS model.

COMMITMENT

Commitment is the cornerstone on which vision is built. It is the desire and dedication by the leader to pursue a given objective or set of objectives or goals for an organization. Commitment can be evidenced in the time a leader invests in his/her work for the organization: devoting more than the required 40 hours at work; devoting time after normal work hours; exhibiting low or no absenteeism; making maximum use of his/her available time; and valuing the time of others through appropriate scheduling. Commitment by the leader is exhibited through the organizational work that he/she accomplishes either individually or as a part of an organizational team. Visibility, availability, and openness to discussion and input are also clear markers of leadership commitment.

A leader who is committed cares about the organization as an entity but also cares about the individuals that make up the organization. Additionally, this leader is concerned about the relationship of the organization and its membership to the people and other organizations external to his/her organization. A committed leader works diligently to balance the needs of the organization with his/her own professional needs, the needs of the members of the organization, and the audience and wider world external to the organization.

SENSE OF DIRECTION

To succeed, a leader must have a clear sense of organizational direction. Initially that sense of direction is embodied in the shared organizational vision. That vision is typically developed when he/she joins the organization or, perhaps, receives an internal promotion and assumes a leadership role within the organization. Just as the leader uses a group process to develop a shared vision, he/she must engage organizational members to devise and carry out a plan to move the organization from where it is toward the vision-based destination. The plan or plans developed will vary tremendously based on the type of enterprise.

But regardless of the enterprise, there are commonalities in leadership behaviors that indicate that he/she has a sense of direction for the organization. The first step most often taken is to develop a strategic plan, followed by development and implementation of action plans. Once the actions plans are operational, monitoring begins. Final steps are assessment of progress and level of success, and realignment as needed.

PROFESSIONALISM

Professionalism provides the lens through which leaders can engage in reflective self-criticism to become better leaders. The same lens allows followers to judge the work-related utterances and actions of the leader. For many leaders their concept of professionalism is based on a code of conduct, professional standards, or code of ethics for their field. Many large organizations memorialize these in official documents.

DECISIVE

Decisiveness is the mechanism by which a leader guides the organization in the direction set forth by the shared vision for the organization. He/she makes decisions that align with that vision and that promote or enhance organizational members' ability to carry out needed tasks in fulfillment of that vision. Those decisions may have minimal observable affect or they may change the course of the organization in radical ways shattering long held beliefs or practices. Regardless of the import of the decision, it is essential to the leader and organizational success that appropriate and timely decisions be made.

WORK ETHIC

As with other aspects of leadership, work ethic is more than what the leader does. He/she is also modeling, leading by example, and inspiring others to develop and exhibit a strong work ethic. Woodward states that "Leadership, organizational and team performance is profoundly influenced by values."[51] That is if the leader places value on a strong work ethic, it is likely that organization members, if they respect and trust the leader, will value a strong work ethic as well.

CONCERN FOR THE FUTURE

Leaders who show concern for the future often include organizational goals and objectives in their vision that will almost surely postdate their tenure. The vison may be for better facilities, more personnel, expansion of services or products, or greater commitment to research and development with an eye toward innovation. Concerned leaders hope to build upon current organizational success and toward the sustainability of organizational success. All leaders have an innate desire to leave an organization in better shape than when they joined it, whether that is through building success, sustaining success, or projecting success into the future.

VISION AND LEADERSHIP

A leader without a vison for the organization he/she leads will surely fail. Vision is truly that critical to overall success as a leader. The vision can be short-term and renewed frequently or long-term with strategic adjustments made at greater intervals, but it must exist. Change is the one constant in life that few, if any, would dispute. Leader vision addresses not only the current tasks but the future of the organization. It is the impetus that generates forward thinking and the ongoing incorporation of new discoveries and innovations. Vision opens the door for the credible, competent, inspirational leader to opportunities for success.

Chapter 7

Route Guidance
Leader Emotional Intelligence

With dynamic route guidance, as opposed to static route guidance,[1] if traffic messages about delays, slow-moving traffic, congestion, or road closures are received, the GPS navigation system checks whether the affected area can be avoided and directs the driver on a newly computed alternative route. Dynamic route guidance provides the most favorable routes available so that traffic flows and congested situations will not occur.

The final destination can be reached with a minimum of delays, difficulty, and rerouting. For leaders, having a dynamic route guidance system is of the utmost importance to success. It will not only provide a means for evaluating the potential for getting to the final destination, if and as the issues arise it will provide the best alternative route.

The GPS model views emotional intelligence (EI) as the source of dynamic route guidance for leaders. Emotional intelligence helps a leader find the right path to follow while taking into account congestion (multiple recommendations for alternate solutions or different visions for the leader and organization), road closures (situations in which cooperation or input is needed but unavailable), and rerouting (the need to be flexible in meeting organizational needs and the needs of organization members as well as consumers). Emotional intelligence enables a credible, competent leader who has the ability to inspire others to engage organizational members in developing and implementing a shared organizational vision.

The research and commentary regarding emotional intelligence paints in broad strokes the importance of this concept. It is the basis for a great deal of the human interaction that occurs in an organization. Daniel Goleman, a widely recognized expert in emotional intelligence holds that "the most effective leaders are alike in one crucial way: they all have a high degree of what has come to be known as emotional intelligence."[2]

This leader GPS imperative was added to the first four as the combined experiences of the authors via anecdotal evidence was overwhelming. Additionally, these findings have been validated over the past two years via the empirical evidence as shared later in this chapter. Furthermore, in this era of technological advances (including the inundation of social media), now, more than ever, skills and training in soft skills are needed. The following pages confirm this notion and are among the most recent literature available.

STAYING GROUNDED: REVISITING EMOTIONAL INTELLIGENCE

Aside from those extremely rare individuals who suffer from alexithymia,[3] all individuals experience emotions individually and in interaction with other individuals. As a leader, the importance of the soft skills of emotional intelligence is twofold. First, a leader must be aware of and capable of controlling his/her emotions (including projecting the proper emotion at the proper time) and also be aware of how his/her projection of emotion is perceived. Second, a leader must be able to distinguish and appropriately relate/respond to the emotions of others. As shared earlier, emotional intelligence is "the basis for a great deal of the human interaction that occurs in an organization.

Recent research related to emotional intelligence and soft skills reinforces the overriding significance of this concept. McKee shared that

> Over the past twenty years, most leaders have come to accept that emotional intelligence is key to their success. But we've still got a long way to go before we realize that developing EQ is a lifelong quest, not an exercise. And for senior leaders and CEOs, who hold people's careers and livelihoods in their hands, it's a responsibility.[4] (p. 2)

Phipps and Prieto support McKee saying that "EI is a complementary interpersonal skill: Yes, intellectual ability and experience are assets for a leader because they can impact his/her competence, which helps facilitate trust. However, an effective leader influences and inspires others to achieve common goals, and thus effective leadership requires people skills."[5] McCarroll relates soft skills this way: "To me, we can sum up soft skills with our attitude, and our relationships with those around us. It is how we make people feel that counts. It is the soft skills that we learn and develop which help us have more empowering relationships."[6]

As they have continued to develop the theoretical and conceptual basis for emotional intelligence, leading researchers in the field Goleman and Boyatzis set forth that emotional intelligence is comprised of "four domains:

self-awareness, self-management, social awareness, and relationship management. Nested within each domain are twelve EI competencies, learned and learnable capabilities that allow outstanding performance at work or as a leader."[7] The competence for self-awareness is emotional self-awareness. For self-management the competencies are emotional self-control, adaptability, achievement orientation, and positive outlook. In the social awareness domain, the competencies are empathy and organizational awareness. And finally, in the relationship management domain, the competencies are influence, coach and mentor, conflict management, teamwork, and inspirational leadership.

Each of the competencies has drawn some attention in research as reflected in the literature as a brief overview will reveal. In a study spanning three years, Eurich found that self-awareness is

> made up of two types of knowledge. One is what people normally think of, which is that introspective awareness, seeing ourselves clearly, knowing what we value, what we aspire to do. But equally importantly and frequently neglected is the idea that we should also know how other people see us. What I found is there are quite a few people who possess one of those types of knowledge, but not the other.[8]

To see where you stand in terms of self-awareness, Meinert suggests that "a 360-degree feedback process can help pinpoint problem areas."[9] The assessment, which uses input from supervisors, colleagues, and subordinates, is often eye-opening. She cautions, however, that a leader might opt for "a more low-profile approach . . . to simply ask trusted colleagues."[10] Interestingly, Eurich finds that "95% of people think they're self-aware, but the real number is closer to 10% to 15%."[11]

Epstein shares that emotional self-awareness can be developed. The path she recommends is to "work to create a team of Loyalists around you, people who trust you, support you, and challenge you to be your best. Surround yourself with people who will speak their truth, even when it's hard. And then listen."[12] Regarding emotional self-control David suggests that

> What we need to do is learn to develop emotional agility, the capacity to mine even the most difficult emotions for data that can help us make better decisions. Managing emotions isn't just doing away with them; it's putting strategies in place that let you use them effectively rather than letting them govern your behaviors and actions. Your emotions are your natural guidance system—and they are more effective when you don't try to fight them.[13]

Adaptability was discussed in chapter 6 and it serves us well to briefly repeat one quote again here for emphasis. Bennis and Thomas stated that "to the extent that any single quality determines success, that quality is adaptive capacity."[14] Current literature is reflective of Bennis and Thomas's 2002 remark.

The Global Leadership Forecast 2018 "integrates data from 25,812 leaders and 2,547 HR professionals across 2,488 organizations" and "spans more than 1,000 C-level executives and 10,000 high-potential employees, includes 54 countries and 26 major industry sectors."[15] The report lists "six competencies that have the greatest impact on performance." The second of those six is *adaptability* about which the report states, "Adaptability is a must. Digital leaders must be able to adapt to constant change or fall behind. They need to be learning every day, not getting caught up in 'traditions.'"[16]

Hero, Lindfors, and Taatila share that "achievement orientation is defined as ambition, the ability to take initiative, goal orientation and generation, learning goal orientation and achievement, and value orientation."[17] In a review of the literature from 2006–2015 they found that "in the collaborative activity of innovation processes a successful participant should have good self-esteem and achievement orientation, be flexible, motivated, and engaged with the task at hand."[18]

Likewise, in a study of self-monitoring and achievement orientation and leader effectiveness, Bastaman, Riantoputra, and Gatari found that "achievement orientation has a significant positive correlation with leader effectiveness."[19] Leaders with a positive, optimistic attitude, as might be expected, tend to generate positive outcomes. For example, from a qualitative study of high school principals, Ceminsky found that positive outlook was identified as "a key theme influencing high levels of job satisfaction."[20]

In a three-part study of the power of positive regard at work, Shefer, Carmeli, and Cohen (2018) found that "when experiencing a high level of regard employees develop a sense of vitality and engage in citizenship behaviours as well as perform their jobs well."[21] Additionally, empathy continues to be a powerful issue with regard to emotional intelligence. As McKee stated, "empathy—the ability to read and understand other's emotions, needs, and thoughts—is one of the core competencies of emotional intelligence and a critical leadership skill."[22] McKee goes on to say that "Developing empathy requires self-awareness, self-management, patience, endurance, and lots and lots of practice but you can learn it with time and dedication."[23]

Goleman defines organizational awareness as "being able to recognize the power relationships, emotional currents, networks, influencers, and dynamics in an organization."[24] Expanding on that definition, Goleman (2017) shares that

> Leaders who can recognize networking opportunities and read key power relationships are better equipped to handle the demands of leadership. Such leaders

not only understand the forces at work in an organization, but also the guiding values and unspoken rules that operate among people. People skilled at the organizational awareness competency can sense the personal networks that make the organization run, and know how to find the right person to make key decisions and how to form a coalition to get something done.[25]

Goleman based that conclusion on a study of organizational change by Battilana and Casciaro who concluded that their personal networks—their relationships with colleagues—were critical.[26] From a study of a large law firm, Casciaro, Gino, and Kouchaki concluded that the individual success of each lawyer "depended on their ability to network effectively both internally (to get themselves assigned to choice clients) and externally (to bring business into the firm)."[27]

While these studies deal with only one aspect of organizational awareness, it is certain that the leader who is more aware of ongoing organizational function and interaction will be more easily able to accomplish the organization's vision. The influence a leader can have is *prima facie case* for ethical leadership and the proper use of the power and authority associated with a leadership role. An example of this influence comes from a study of senior leader influence on corporate social responsibility by Reimer, Van Doorn, and Heyden who share that "in general, our empirical results support the relevance of the interaction between CEOs (chief executive officer) and their TMTs (top management teams) in defining their firms' CSR (corporate social responsibility) profile."[28]

Coaching and mentoring were discussed in detail in chapter 1. Of mentoring, we shared it is a first critical step to seeking willing mentors who are themselves successful leaders in your field. As we have shared before, conflict is a natural human experience that can either have a positive or negative effect. The emotionally intelligent leader attempts to resolve conflicts, if possible with a win-win approach. One way to do so is illustrated in a study of how a supervisor can help subordinates resolve relationship conflict (RC) by Thiel, Griffith, Hardy, Peterson, and Connelly. They share that "an effective way of resolving escalated RC is to help subordinates reappraise events that led to the conflict in a less affectively threatening way."[29]

Given the nature of leadership (that it requires followers), it seems sensible that teamwork (interpersonal interactions in the GPS model) would be included in a discussion of emotional intelligence. Koeslag-Kreunen, Van den Bossche, Hoven, Van der Klink, and Gijselaers, in a study of team learning, found, not surprisingly, that "person-focused leaders foster team learning for both adaptive and developmental tasks, whereas task-focused leaders influence team learning for adaptive tasks only."[30] Valuing people has value for the leader and the organization.

In chapter 5, inspirational leadership was discussed in detail. A quote from Garton and Mankins was included and is worth repeating:

> Most of us know how important inspiration can be in everyday life. In the workplace, as one pundit put it, employees react differently when they encounter a wall. Satisfied employees hold a meeting to discuss what to do about walls. Engaged employees begin looking around for ladders to scale the wall. Inspired employees break right through it.[31]

The above twelve competencies without doubt lay a framework for research in emotional intelligence and its applicability to leadership. But other areas of interest are also emerging in relation to emotional intelligence.

One such topic that has emerged more recently in association with emotional intelligence is mindfulness. Goleman and Lippincott said of mindfulness,

> Mindfulness is a method of shifting your attention inward to observe your thoughts, feelings, and actions without interpretation or judgment. A mindfulness practice often begins simply by focusing on your breath, noticing when your mind wanders, and then bringing it back to your breath. As you strengthen your ability to concentrate, you can then shift to simply noting your inner experience without getting lost in it at any point in your day. The benefits attributed to this kind of practice range from stronger relationships with others to higher levels of leadership performance.[32]

Distinguishing what mindfulness is and is not, Goleman shared that,

> Here's the bottom line: While you shouldn't believe everything you hear about mindfulness, there are, indeed, payoffs from a meditation habit. In fact, the research also shows that more hours of meditation you put in over your lifetime, the better the results on the forefronts we've described. Think of mindfulness as a way to enhance certain kinds of mental fitness, just as regular workouts at the gym build physical fitness.[33]

Other researchers' findings support Goleman. For example, in a study of mindfulness and leader flexibility, Rouleau, Grégoire, and Baron found four of the five dimensions of mindfulness (nonreactivity, nonjudging, acting with awareness, and describing) were positively correlated with the overall flexibility score of emotional intelligence.[34] Other areas that align with emotional intelligence may also emerge over time.

Nonetheless, whether expressed through one of Goleman and Boyatzis's four domains or through the supporting characteristics, we share as associated the GPS imperative emotional intelligence and soft skills (resilience, communication and listening, happiness, personality traits—specifically the big traits such as sense of humor, assertiveness, flexibility, or empathy and interpersonal interactions); emotional intelligence and soft skills are omnipresent intrapersonal and interpersonal phenomena that drive leader success.

Leaders should heed two forms of advice regarding emotional intelligence. First, leaders should be cognizant that emotional intelligence can positively impact leader–follower interaction. Second, and just as importantly, leaders must be cognizant that emotional intelligence can have a negative influence on leader–follower interaction. The latter occurs when the use of emotional intelligence is inappropriate. As Bacon shares, "there is a growing body of evidence suggesting a darker side to trait EI and several studies have suggested that it may be used as a tool for deception or manipulative relational behaviours."[35]

Carucci supports this when he says that there are "manipulative misuses of emotional intelligence—the intentionally subtle regulating of one's emotions to engineer responses from others that might not be in their best interest."[36] He shares three specific manipulative behaviors to beware of: "a need to be the hero disguised as 'empathy'; a need to be right masquerading as 'active listening'; and, a need for approval dressed up as 'self-awareness.'"[37] Leaders with Leadership Acumen use their emotional intelligence to produce positive outcomes and avoid the pitfalls and potential derailment brought on misuse of emotional intelligence.

Again, referring back to the crux of emotional intelligence and soft skills, as Goleman so eloquently put it,

> it's not that IQ and technical skills are irrelevant. They do matter, but mainly as "threshold capabilities"; that is, they are the entry-level requirements for executive positions. But my research, along with other recent studies, clearly shows that emotional intelligence is the *sine qua non* of leadership. Without it, a person can have the best training in the world, an incisive, analytical mind, and an endless supply of smart ideas, but he still won't make a great leader.[38]

It is also the means by which a leader can sharply increase his/her leader acumen. In the leader GPS model emotional intelligence is based on resilience, communication, and listening skills, happiness, sense of humor, personality traits, assertiveness, flexibility, and empathy in interpersonal interactions. The following sections detail the contributions of each of these components to a leader's emotional intelligence.

RESILIENCE

Resilience is the hallmark of a leader with high emotional intelligence. But what exactly is resilience? The definitions vary but share the common threads of adaptation, perseverance, and tenacity in the face of stress and/or adversity. Contu[39] said of resilience, "It is merely the skill and the capacity to be robust under conditions of enormous stress and change." For Margolis and Stoltz, "resilience is the capacity to respond quickly and constructively to crises."[40]

A resilient leader then is able to cope with any situation that occurs. He/she controls the situation rather than the situation controlling him/her. As Stoltz put it, "Over the course of your years, either adversity consumes you, or you consume it."[41] Or as Thomas related, "Resilience, a central facet of adaptive capacity, makes it possible for leaders to find calm in the face of tension and to begin the search for answers."[42] But what is the source of a leader's resilience?

COMMUNICATION AND LISTENING

Communication is one of the most powerful tools a leader possesses. In what he/she says and does (not all communication is verbal) a leader establishes the legitimacy of his/her role as a leader. Goleman lists communication as one of the primary social skills of an emotionally intelligent leader and defines communication as "skill at listening and at sending clear, convincing, and well-tuned messages."[43]

Listening as a critical skill often does not receive the attention it deserves. Keyser states that

> Successful leaders assert that listening is a key factor to their effectiveness.
> These executives actively probe and challenge the information they receive so they can build a strong knowledge base of fresh ideas and insights. Unfortunately, the art of active listening often is overlooked when compared with the other business acumen skills that executives must demonstrate in their day-to-day work and interactions.[44]

HAPPINESS

Happiness is an internal, emotional state of mind. It is that place and point in time where consciously, in a reflective moment, but more often unconsciously, an individual is at peace with himself/herself and is at peace with the people and daily events in his/her life. He/she is satisfied and enjoys a sense of wholeness, comfort, and well-being.

Simply put, happiness is an individual characteristic and can only be assessed by the individual himself/herself. Furthermore, happiness for any individual is based on the totality of his/her life circumstance. However, happiness or satisfaction with any one aspect of a person's life such as his/her work can be assessed though the assessment is still subjective and applies only to that individual.

SENSE OF HUMOR

Former president of the United States, Dwight D. Eisenhower, is credited with saying "A sense of humor is part of the art of leadership, of getting along with people, of getting things done."[45] He was right across the board. Leadership, like teaching, is art applied scientifically. And, two of the primary characteristics of a great leader are the ability to get along with people and being able to get things done. Eisenhower's quip is supported by research.

As Sala shared, "More than four decades of study by various researchers confirms some common-sense wisdom: Humor, used skillfully, greases the management wheels. It reduces hostility, deflects criticism, relieves tension, improves morale, and helps communicate difficult messages."[46] Similarly, a study by the Bell Leadership Group found that "when employees are asked to describe the strengths and weaknesses of senior colleagues in their organizations, "'sense of humor' and 'work ethic' are mentioned twice as much as any other phrases."[47]

PERSONALITY TRAITS

A person is defined by their individual personality. Like a fingerprint, it is theirs and theirs alone. Personality is what makes each of us who we are. It also defines to a great extent our interaction with others. Psychological research provides us a clear schematic of the attributes of personality in the five-factor model.

However, a full recitation of the development of the five-factor model is beyond the scope of this discussion but based on the work of William McDouglall, Tupes, Christal, Cattell, Digman, and many others, a consensus as to the predominate traits from which personality forms and finds expression has been developed and is widely accepted. As Digman shared in 1990, "the past decade has witnessed a rapid convergence of views regarding the structure of the concepts of personality (i.e. the language of personality)."

The five-factor model rests on the tenet that the attributes of "extraversion/introversion (or surgency), friendliness/hostility (or agreeableness), conscientiousness (or will), neuroticism/emotional stability (or emotional stability), and intellect (or openness)" are the primary factors that determine personality.[104] Even with consensus on the importance of these factors, of course, there still remains substantial debate as to whether or to what extent personality is inherited or developed/learned, the nature of nurture conundrum and the extent/weight of the contribution of each factor to the personality of any given individual. Maccorby shares, "An effective leader recognizes personality differences, but succeeds in creating a common sense of purpose, a shared identity as members of a team."[48]

ASSERTIVENESS

From a leadership perspective, to move an organization forward leaders must assert themselves. Learning how to be assertive in an effective manner is based in large part on a leader's ability to gauge the existing emotional situation and emotional impact of his/her actions. Santora stated that "one of the characteristics that people sometimes look for in leaders is assertiveness. But where should leaders draw the line when it comes to assertiveness?"[49] Santora based his answer to that question on the results of a study by Ames and Flynn who found that

> The present research confirmed our expectation that individual differences in assertiveness are a critical component of perceptions of leadership and that the link between assertiveness and leadership is not as simple as was suggested by prior reports of positive or negative linear effects. References to assertiveness dominated perceptions about the weaknesses of potential leaders, having appeared as a clear theme in as many as half of the coworker comments, far more frequently than references to other commonly studied attributes, including intelligence, conscientiousness, and charisma.[50]

More simply put, leaders who display moderate levels of assertiveness are more well accepted than those at either extreme who are overly assertive or lack assertiveness.

FLEXIBILITY

In juxtaposition to assertiveness is flexibility. The constant flux of any enterprise calls for leaders to be flexible. As Good and Sharma share, "Leader flexibility can be a pivotal aspect of leadership development."[51] In the same vein, Yukl states that "Research on leadership and management during the past several decades provide strong evidence that flexible, adaptive leadership is essential for most managers."[52]

But what constitutes flexibility? Aaker and Mascarenhas provide the classic definition: "flexibility represents the 'ability of the organization to adapt to substantial, uncertain and fast occurring (relative to the required reaction time) environmental changes that have a meaningful impact on the organization's performance.'"[53] Other, more recent definitions describe flexibility in terms of adaptability. Soffer says, "Basically, flexibility is described as capability to react to uncertainty by adaptation."[54] Other aspects of flexibility include a willingness to allow broad latitude in decision-making and allowing latitude to employees in their work schedule.

EMPATHY AND INTERPERSONAL INTERACTIONS

What is empathy and how does a leader display empathy? Goleman says of empathy:

> empathy doesn't mean a kind of "I'm okay, you're okay" mushiness. For a leader, that is, it doesn't mean adopting other people's emotions as one's own and trying to please everybody. That would be a nightmare—it would make action impossible. Rather, empathy means thoughtfully considering employees' feelings—along with other factors—in the process of making intelligent decisions. Empathy is particularly important today as a component of leadership for at least three reasons: the increasing use of teams; the rapid pace of globalization; and the growing need to retain talent.[55]

In the leader GPS model empathy is also the gateway to strong interpersonal relationships. Leaders by definition have followers (for leaders that means organizational members and/or consumers of the product or service the organization produces or offers). Research has shown with some clarity that leaders who are able to establish a firm bond of trust and respect with both internal and external constituencies of an organization produce positive results.

Warren Bennis said it this way: "great leaders earn respect, daily, and build and maintain trust with all constituents."[56] Emotional intelligence promotes the development of trust and respect through leader display of empathy in the interpersonal interactions that make up the majority of the work in his/her routine day. A leader with high LSA will also display high emotional intelligence.

EMOTIONAL INTELLIGENCE AND LEADERSHIP

The emergence of emotional intelligence as a prime driving force in leadership gives added emphasis to the importance soft skills described to this point that support credibility, competence, inspiration, vision. People are rational but also emotional beings. They often react as much or more with their hearts as they do with their minds. The leader who, through developing his/her leader acumen, can also master the ability to recognize and react appropriately to both the rational and emotional sides of an individual has a decided advantage over the leader who lacks those abilities. When, in addition, a leader has a firm grasp of his/her own rational and emotional sides, he/she greatly expands the likelihood of success for himself/herself, the individuals within the organization and the organization itself.

Chapter 8

"Updating Your Internal GPS"
Building Leadership Acumen

THE IMPORTANCE OF BUILDING LEADERSHIP CAPACITY

As you may have discerned at this point, some or perhaps several of the GPS constructs you are already comfortable with or are relatively familiar to you. In like manner, as a driver, there are places you regularly "go" for which you need no assistance. For these trips as well as local ones around town, you may never need to engage your GPS. Once you learn a route, it can become second nature, practically like turning on "auto-pilot" to return to this destination.

Similarly, in those Leader GPS components in which you are confident, you simply continue to move forward with "map" updates as needed. However, with the realization that you may need additional information in some area, you might—in a metaphorical sense—decide to engage the GPS for assistance.

Analogously, for all leaders, even those with seemingly innate leadership ability, the Leader GPS must be occasionally updated. This is the result of training, imprinting (hopefully in an organization with leaders who excel), and active learning in all situations. It is a coming together of skills that can be learned. The Leader GPS must also be constantly reinforced and broadened in depth and scope as changes occur in the circumstances of the leader, the organization of which he/she is a part, and the environment (the global world) in which the organization exists.

The primary rationale for building Leader Acumen is that a leader be open to learning—learning leadership as a student while in postsecondary education or perhaps earlier and learning on the job when he/she enters the work world. Without a predisposition toward leadership, development of leader acumen may be slow and the progress toward mastery of the skills related to the leader GPS may be sporadic at best. In addition to being open to learning, a leader must actively seek out learning opportunities.

The first of those opportunities comes in assessing one's relative strengths and weaknesses (areas for growth). The authors of this work have devised such a measure in the form of a 360-type assessment. This assessment (as described in earlier chapters) may be used alone as a tool for self-reflection but is more effectively utilized with feedback from others.

A second opportunity for learning and growth is having a mentor. As Bennis points out regarding mentoring, "The best mentors are usually recruited, and one mark of a future leader is the ability to identify, woo, and win the mentors who will change his or her life."[1] Bennis's point is well taken. Everyone has been around people who have knowledge that would be beneficial to others. But how many have taken the time to seek out or create opportunities for those individuals to share the knowledge they have?

The inquisitive, curious, and determined (one might say "dogged") among those new to a field of endeavor (or even those long term in a field who want to expand their horizons) may be a step ahead. They establish relationships with peers and superiors that allow them access to the knowledge they seek and the learning opportunities that knowledge brings. Without necessarily calling them mentors, they have established a mentoring relationship.

Another learning opportunity is found through imprinting. This type of learning occurs in a different manner than mentoring. Imprinting occurs during a sensitive period when an individual first joins an organization or when he/she moves to a different position within that organization or even to another organization. It occurs through observation and/or interaction with others within the organization. Simply put, aspiring leaders are imprinted individually with skills and dispositions exhibited by those organizational leaders and peers.

And, that imprinting is reflective of the knowledge and practices within that organization in general. This type of learning is heuristic in nature occurring as the observer attempts to make sense of the steps taken to answer a question or reach a goal or objective. And, unlike mentoring it may not involve direct contact with the individual. The imprinting may be based more on the ambience and/or practices of the organization. Higgins, who calls this career imprinting, said "an organizational career imprint is the set of capabilities and connections, coupled with the confidence and cognition that a group of individuals share as a result of their career experiences at a common employer during a particular period in time."[2]

Whether the imprint is individual or organizational, the knowledge transferred or learned helps to build LSA. Having seen and or/experienced what works and what does not work, a leader has a broader and more refined repertoire of responses and possible solutions to issues and problems and additionally the resource base to contemplate innovative solutions or to create totally new solutions.

A fourth type of learning opportunity is imprinting via extended training or professional development. This is the type of learning typically associated with those who are lifelong learners or, at least, with those who are in professions that require continuing education for renewal of licenses or certification in latest techniques.

A leader who stops learning and does not progress will almost certainly fail at some point. The changing global environment that reaches into the smallest and most obscure corner of any enterprise will render old knowledge obsolete and the leader with it. Once again proactive seeking of learning opportunities is essential. Find those learning opportunities that have the potential to affect you individually and avail yourself of them.

A final but equally important type of learning is critical self-reflection. Polizzi and Frick state that "Critical self-reflection and engagement with the experiences and critical incidents of one's life is essential."[3] McAlpin and Weston shared regarding teachers engaging in reflective practice that "Ongoing use of the process of reflection is essential for building knowledge, and increasing knowledge increases one's ability to use reflection effectively and to develop as a teacher."[4] Their statement applies equally well to leaders. Friedman perhaps said it best

> Becoming a better leader requires constant reflection—making sense of your experience and then discovering ways to use your insights to increase your impact. Then, to stay ever sharp, it's good to teach what you've learned (and then try to teach what you still *want* to learn). Learning leadership by doing it—what's called *action learning*, which is what you've been engaged in through your efforts with this book—is effective only when you take the time to reflect on what worked, what didn't work, and what you might do differently in the future. Looking back is a necessary step in the process of learning and performance improvement in which you've invested much so far. If you give short shrift to the task of reflection, then the lessons don't get internalized. They don't last.[5]

This internalization of learning allows the final step in Maslow's hierarchy of needs—self-actualization. As Maslow said about self-actualization, "What a man *can* be, he *must* be. This need we may call self-actualization."[6] It is by this process that leaders, and followers, gain the greatest insight into their own character, skills, and abilities. Critical reflection is also the means by which a leader develops a vision for an organization and sets about establishing the resources and tasks needed to achieve that vision.

The first three learning opportunities represent the external influence on learning and the reliance on others. Reliance on others for learning opportunities is the norm. But self-reliance in seeking learning opportunities is also important whether through reflection, seeking mentors, learning via imprinting by being cognizant of opportunities when observing leaders or organizational functioning, or critical self-reflection.

As Turesky and Wood state, "we have concluded that leadership development is a highly individual learning process."[7] As Korthagen shared about reflective practice, "It is vital that employees learn how to manage their own development, so that they learn from each new experience, and become ever more proficient at independently integrating new insights into their day-to-day activities."[8] Aspiring leaders must be proactive in seeking the knowledge they need to apply the skills they learn.

The resourceful aspiring leader will use all of the types of learning opportunities. He/she will be a lifelong learner and will use what he/she has learned to navigate the leadership challenges he/she will face. The leader will also realize that all of the elements of the Leader GPS interact with one another to produce the characteristics and skills that define them as a leader. This leader will come to have a quite advanced internalized GPS that utilizes these elements to steer a true course to success.

PRELIMINARY RESEARCH FINDINGS

The Assessments

During the course of the 2016–17 and 2017–18 school years, the authors provided the Leader/Educator Assessment (LEA) (both self and circle) and leadership development training (LEAD) to school district leaders in a large county school district in the southeastern United States. The group consisted of forty-nine principals (two specialty schools, twenty-nine elementary schools, ten middle schools, and eight high schools). Additionally, eight central office staff who served in various positions participated in the assessments and training. All participants were given the LEA short form to begin the sessions and again at the end. The administrations were approximately one year apart. The first administration was in the spring of the 2016–17 school year; the second in the spring of the 2017–18 school year.

The LEA short form consists of 33 paired semantic differential items based the five leader GPS leadership imperatives. The circle/360 group included 1,828 faculty and staff respondents. The LEA short form provides scores for each leader GPS imperative (Credibility, Competence, Ability to Inspire, Vision, and Emotional Intelligence/Soft Skills) as well as an LEA Total Score, which is the sum of the individual imperatives.

Leader GPS Imperative Training

The training provided by the authors to school district principals and central office staff was threefold. The primary approach included the use of presenting Situational Judgment Tests (SJTs) from *Growing Your Leadership-Scenarios from Practicing K12 Administrators or Soft Skills for Leaders-Scenarios from Higher Education Administrators*.[9] Much as in the traditional administration of SJTs, the participants were given very brief scenarios (with a leadership bent) along with multiple choice answer options as solutions. Prior to providing option responses, the participants were asked to briefly pen a solution on a 3 × 5 index card. Participants (in small groups) were allowed to discuss the scenarios and then required to come to consensus regarding a solution to the SJT.

Additionally, large group dialogue was employed. These exercises help to develop their leadership and decision-making skills. A second aspect of the training was providing the group with practical suggestions for behaviors and steps to take that are associated with each leader GPS imperative and the related subcategories of each imperative. This provided a useful, employable means to address concerns/weaknesses in any area on the LEA self-assessment or the LEA circle/360 assessment. The third aspect was to have them implement the practices they felt would address their relative weaknesses. In relation to this third aspect, the participants were also required to write and submit a reflective piece regarding what they had gained from the LEAD training and how they further intended to use it.

QUANTITATIVE FINDINGS

Quantitative Findings for Principals

The results of the first administration of the LEA self-assessment for the district principals' group indicated that the Credibility score was the highest leader self-score among the five leadership imperatives. For the first administration, the remaining GPS imperative scores in order were competence, vision, ability to inspire, and emotional intelligence/soft skills. Credibility, then, was viewed by district principals as their strongest leadership characteristic with emotional intelligence being the weakest characteristic.

The results of the second administration of the LEA self-assessment for the district principals' group reflected again that the Credibility average was the highest leader self-score among the five leadership imperatives. For the second administration, however, the order of the remaining imperative scores were slightly different. In order, those scores were vision (moved up one place from third to second), competence (moved down one place from second to third), and in like fashion, ability to inspire and emotional intelligence/soft skills change places from fifth to fourth and fourth to fifth, respectively. Credibility, then, continued to be viewed by district principals as their strongest leadership characteristic with ability to inspire being the weakest characteristic.

Comparison of the LEA self-assessment for the district principals' group for all GPS imperatives indicated that the leader self-scores decreased for all imperatives and the LEA total score between administration one and two. The across the board decrease in leader self-score from the first administration of the LEA to the second administration of the LEA was anticipated. After the leaders received the circle scores and recognized the dissonance (lack of congruence) between the self-scores and the circle scores, they tended to reassess. This self-perception resulted in lower LEA self-scores on the second administration. However, only the difference in the leader self-scores for competence between the two LEA administrations revealed a small but statistically significant difference.

The results of the first administration of the LEA circle/360 test for the district principals' group indicated that the Credibility average was the highest leader self-score among the five leadership imperatives. For the first administration, the remaining GPS imperative scores ranked in order were vision, competence, ability to inspire, and emotional intelligence/soft skills. Credibility then was also viewed by the CIRCLES of these principals as their strongest leadership characteristic with emotional intelligence being the weakest characteristic.

The results of the second administration of the LEA circle/360 for the district principals' group indicated that the Credibility average was again the highest leader self-score among the five leadership imperatives. For the second administration, the order of the remaining GPS imperative scores were identical to the first administration.

Comparison of the LEA circle/360 for the first and second administrations revealed an increase for all imperatives. The across the board increase in leader self-score from the first administration of the LEA to the second administration of the LEA was a desirable outcome but not one that was anticipated. The faculty and staff participants were not apprised of the dissonance (lack of congruence) between the self-scores. The faculty and staff responses to the second administration therefore *were due to a change in the participants' perception of the leader*. While the improvement in congruence is encouraging and speaks to the change in faculty and staff perception and to the effort expended by the leader to change, none of the differences rose to the level of statistically significance but should be considered as emergent growth.

LEAD training played a part in the changes noted in the second administration of the LEA self and circle/360 assessments. Those results, as stated above, indicated that leaders tended to reassess their self-perception and the circle/360 participants (the faculty and staff working with each principal) responded with higher ratings of their leader and a closer congruence of perception of the leader based on the GPS imperatives. Growth was shown albeit the growth statistically speaking was not significant numerically.

Quantitative Findings for Central Office Leaders

The results of the first administration of the LEA leader self-assessment for the district central office group indicated that the Credibility average was the highest leader self-score among the five leadership imperatives. For the first administration, the remaining GPS imperative scores in order were emotional intelligence/soft skills, competence, vision, and ability to inspire. Credibility then was viewed by district central office group as their strongest leadership characteristic with ability to inspire being the weakest characteristic.

The results of the second administration of the LEA leader self-assessment for the district central office group indicated that the Credibility average was again the highest leader self-score among the five leadership imperatives. For the second administration, however, the order of the remaining GPS imperative scores were slightly different. In order those scores were vision (moved up two places from fourth to second), emotional intelligence/soft skills (moved down one place from second to third), competence (moved down one place from third to fourth), and ability to inspire, which did not change place. Credibility then continued to be viewed by central office group as their strongest leadership characteristic with ability to inspire being the weakest characteristic.

Comparison of the self LEA for the district central office group for all GPS imperatives for the first and second administrations of the LEA short form indicated that the central office group self-scores decreased for all imperatives. The across the board decrease in leader self-score from the first administration of the LEA to the second administration of the LEA was anticipated. Once the central office group received the circle scores and recognized the dissonance (lack of congruence) between the self-scores and the circle scores, they tended to reassess their self-perception, which resulted in lower LEA self-scores on the second administration. However, none of the differences in the central office participants' self-scores between the two LEA administrations was statistically significant.

The results of the first administration of the LEA circle/360 for the district central office group indicated that the Credibility average was the highest leader self-score among the five leadership imperatives. For the first administration, the remaining GPS imperative scores in order were competence, vision, emotional intelligence/soft skills, and ability to inspire. Credibility then was viewed by the central office group as their strongest leadership characteristic with ability to inspire being the weakest characteristic.

The results of the second administration of the LEA circle/360 for the district central office group indicated that the Credibility average was again the highest leader self-score among the five leadership imperatives. For the second administration, the order of the remaining GPS imperative scores were identical to the first administration. In order those scores were competence, vision, emotional intelligence/soft skills, and ability to inspire. Credibility then continued to be viewed by district principals as their strongest leadership characteristic with ability to inspire being the weakest characteristic.

Comparison of the LEA circle/360 for the district central office group for all GPS imperatives for the first and second administrations of the LEA short form indicated that the circle/360 scores increased for all imperatives. The across the board increase in leader self-score from the first administration of the LEA to the second administration of the LEA was a desirable outcome but not one that was anticipated. While the improvement in congruence is encouraging and speaks to the change in faculty and staff perception and to the effort expended by the leader to change (perhaps due at least in part to his/her LEAD training), none of the differences in the circle/360 scores between the two LEA administrations was statistically significant.

As with the principals' group LEAD training played a part in the changes noted in the second administration of the LEA self and circle/360 assessments for the central office group. Those results, as stated above, indicated that leaders tended to reassess their self-perception and the circle/360 participants (the faculty/staff working with each central office member) responded with higher ratings of their leader and a closer congruence of perception of the leader based on the leader GPS imperatives. Growth was shown albeit that the growth in general was not statistically significant.

QUALITATIVE FINDINGS

The qualitative findings come from three questions: one asked to the leaders and two asked to the circle/360 participants. The question for the leaders was: what have I done or what will I do to improve my leader perception in the minds of the faculty and staff? The two questions asked of the circle/360 participants were as follows. What is the best leadership quality or strength of the *leader* you have just rated? What is the main area for leadership growth and improvement you would recommend for this *leader*?

Qualitative Findings for Leaders (Principals and Central Office Staff)

A sample of the leader responses illuminates their efforts to improve the faculty and staff perception of their leadership.

- I have focused on being optimistic with a most positive tone.
- One other specific action I have implemented is to ask others for their opinion and listen more.
- My staff and I have worked hard to increase our school's credibility in the community.
- I have learned over the past year that I do not know everything.
- I have learned that it is okay to ask for knowledge and insight from peers and mentors.
- I have worked to be more conscious and intentional in my behavior and actions.
- This year I have made an effort to recognize and celebrate my staff's accomplishments and hard work.
- I try to communicate more with the faculty.
- . . . focus on tasks that inspire and encourage my teachers.
- I will continue to work with staff in daily interactions, share concerns more openly, and explain the direction I will take in actions.
- Make time to speak to each staff personally.
- The skillset I would like to focus on for the next few months is soft skills. I have been known to be direct and not so compassionate.
- I am asking for feedback so that I can better create a team atmosphere.
- I will try to respond to emails in a timelier manner.

It is clear from this sampling that the intent of the leaders was to reach out to faculty and staff members and to engage them more fully both individually and organizationally. Such steps by the leaders resulted in the increase in circle/360 ratings the leaders received.

Qualitative Findings from the Leaders' CIRCLEs

Repeated again here for clarity, the two questions asked of the circle/360 participants were as follows. What is the best leadership quality or strength of the *leader* you have just rated? What is the main area for leadership growth/improvement you would recommend for this *leader*?

As the respondents were guaranteed anonymity, they answered with candor. A sample of the responses to the two questions appear in Tables 8.1 and 8.2. The responses are divided based on the LEA CIRCLE score of the leaders.

Table 8.1 Circle Responses for Top Ranked Leaders*

What does my leader do best?	In what area could my leader grow?
Compassionate (concerned/caring)	Being more personable/friendlier
Visionary	Take time for themselves
Passionate	Delegate more
Determined	
Involved/Engaged	
Knowledgeable	

* As ranked by the state report card.

Table 8.2 Circle Responses for Bottom Ranked Leaders*

What does my leader do best?	In what area could my leader grow?
Compassionate (concerned/caring/friendly)	Student Discipline
Positive/Optimistic	Involvement/Being Engaged
Helpful	Energy/Enthusiasm
Supportive/Encouraging	Caring/Passion/Understanding
Considerate/Understanding	
Involved/Engaged	

* As ranked by the state report card.

These scores are divided into a top scoring group (their CIRCLEs rated them very positively) and a bottom scoring group (whose CIRCLEs rated them poorly on the quantitative scale).

In the top scoring group, the comments described the best qualities or strengths of leaders as compassion (concern and caring), vision, passion, determination, involvement/engagement, and knowledge. This same group, however, described some of the leaders as needing growth in the areas of being personable and friendlier. The comments also included the suggestion that the leader should take time for himself/herself (overly strong task orientation) and that the leader needed to delegate more.

For the bottom scoring group, the comments described the best qualities or strengths of leaders as displaying compassion (concern and caring), having a positive and optimistic attitude, being helpful, supportive, and encouraging, being considerate and understanding, and being involved and engaged. Growth areas for the bottom scoring leaders include improving student discipline, being more involved and engaged, showing more energy/enthusiasm, and being more caring, passionate, and understanding.

As can been seen, there are commonalities between and among the groups. These commonalities spell out with some clarity the perceptions of the leaders' skillsets but also indicate with equal clarity the characteristics that teachers are looking for in their leaders.

ANECDOTAL IMPRESSIONS

In working closely with a group for over a year, impressions are formed and verified or cast aside. The following are impressions we came away with from our year's work with the group. Through reading, assessment, and reflection, many administrators have

- come to know their strengths better;
- identified areas of weaknesses;
- become more aware of their faculty's perceptions of their leadership;
- worked to improve;
- acknowledged the importance of their roles; and
- engendered a better sense and understanding of engaging the faculty and staff.

As shared in the preface, one interesting, yet not surprising, finding of our work with leaders from various fields is that *confidence tempered with humility* is the resounding consequence and ultimate branding of leadership at its most effective—the level of true leader acumen. The final impressions we formed from the year's work is that LSA can be taught, is sensitive to instruction, and can be increased through acting on self-critical reflection. Mentoring was not a factor for this group, though we still believe that mentoring would bring greater positive results. It is also clear that further research is needed. We are undertaking that work during the 2018–19 school year as we work with a new statewide group of K–12 educational leaders, a university level group of leaders, and many various practicing or aspiring leaders all of whom will also have a mentor working with them.

Chapter 9
"A Rough Road"
Avoiding Leadership Derailment

Ever been traveling down a busy road and encountered a person walking along the side of the road with a gas can in his/her hand? It's hard to believe that even with all of the technological advances, warning lights, ringing bells, and gauges that someone in this day and age could run out of gas. But it happens. When this happens, the "journey" takes a back seat to the immediate "derailment." Sometimes, a short walk, a full can of gas, and the driver is back on the road. For others, it may not be as simple. Perhaps the opportunity to get a fuel refill is quite far away. Worse yet, something more could complicate the initial trip to get fuel.

In spite of the capabilities of an updated GPS, it still does not have the power to force the driver to stop and get gas. Only the driver has the capacity to make that determination. Neither can the automobile choose to do so on its own. The only way for a successful *true north* journey is with an astute driver. Derailment can happen and it happens at the hand of the leader.

LEADERSHIP DERAILMENT

Chapter 3 contained a brief discussion dealing with leadership failure as it relates to credibility. That discussion focused on three categories of leaders who fail: those who commit unlawful acts; those who commit questionable acts; and, those who are derailed. Leaders in the first two categories, with rare exceptions, lose credibility and no longer lead. Those leaders made poor choices and paid the price for those choices. Leaders in the third category, derailed leaders, often find another chance to lead. So, what exactly is derailment?

Derailment, which has been extensively examined in business research, is defined in a variety of ways. For Beaumont, "Derailment is said to have happened when leaders—who may have shown a good record of success and who seem to possess the necessary skills, abilities and knowledge to succeed—suddenly and spectacularly fail."[1] The Center for Creative Leadership shared that

> A derailed manager is one who, having reached the general manager level, is fired, demoted, or reaches a career plateau. It's important to note that organizations saw the derailed managers as having high potential for advancement, as having impressive track records, and holding a solidly established leadership position—until they derailed. Derailment doesn't refer to individuals who have topped out in their company's hierarchy or to managers who elect to stay at a particular level.[2]

Van Velsor and Ascalon offer a somewhat similar definition: "A derailed executive is one who, having reached the general manager level, finds that there is little chance of future advancement due to a misfit between job requirements and personal skills. The executive is either plateaued or leaves the organization altogether."[3] From Burke, "Derailment in a leadership or executive role is defined as being involuntarily plateaued, demoted or fired below the level of expected achievement or reaching that level but unexpectedly failing."[4] Furnham in his seminal work on leader failure found that

> The work on leaders who fail is marked by a number of different terms. The choice of the terms seems relatively arbitrary and the personal favourite of a writer or of people in a particular discipline. Technically they do have slightly different meanings. The following is an incomplete list from an ever-growing group of words used in this area.
>
> - **Aberrant (leaders)** This emphasizes abnormality, atypicality, and deviance from the right or normal type. It has two themes: both unusualness and also a departure from acceptable standards. That is, it has a statistical *and* moral side to it.
> - **Anti-social (leaders)** This echoes the immoral nature of leaders who can be anti-social in the way selfish people may be, but more likely the way delinquents are anti-social. More importantly, perhaps, it echoes the new term for psychopath: anti-social personality disorder.
> - **Dark side (Triad) (leaders)** This is to contrast the bright and the dark; the outside, the obvious and the straightforward with the inside, the obscure and the devious. Dark implies evil, dismal, and menacing. The triad suggests three separable constituents of evil.
> - **Derailed (leaders)** This emphasizes the idea of being thrown off course. Trains on tracks derail. Leaders set fair in a particular direction deviate from

the path, unable to move forward. It is sometimes hyphenated with the next word in the dictionary, namely *deranged* which implies not only a breakdown in performance but also insanity.
- **Despotic (leaders)** This is taken from the historical literature emphasizing the misuse and abuse of power by oppressive, absolutist leaders. It emphasizes the autocratic type or style of leadership.
- **Destructive (leaders)** Used by historians in this context to look at the impact of a particular leadership style, it speaks of the ruining, spoiling, or neutralizing of a group or force led by a particular person.
- **Incompetent (leaders)** This is used to suggest inadequate, ineffective, unqualified. It implies the absence of something required rather than the presence of something not required. Incompetent leaders are ineffective because they are lacking in particular qualities.
- **Malignant (leaders)** These are leaders who spread malevolence, the antonym of benevolence. Malevolence is misconduct, doing harm such as maliciously causing pain or damage. Malignant leaders, like cancer, grow fast and are deadly.
- **Toxic (leaders)** This refers to the poisonous effect leaders have on all they touch. Toxic substances kill rather than repel. Again, this refers to the consequences of a particular leadership style.
- **Tyrannical (leaders)** Tyrants show arbitrary, oppressive, and unjust behaviour. Tyrants tend to usurp power and then brutally oppress those they command.[5]

The common theme in these definitions is that an up and coming, promising leader at some point is no longer able to lead successfully. The leader has risen through the ranks, paid his/her dues, mastered his/her trade or profession to a point in time, is seen as having leadership potential, and is elevated to a leadership position. Then he/she fails as a leader. But, how does derailment happen?

Van Velsor and Leslie, in their review, of derailment found that "there are four enduring themes. They are present, both over time and across countries. They include problems with interpersonal relationships; failure to meet business objectives; failure to build and lead a team; inability to change or adapt during a transition."[6]

A range of opinions exist as to the causes of derailment. Hogan and Hogan related that "We believe failure is more related to having undesirable qualities than lacking desirable ones."[7] Hogan, citing Bentz, said that Bentz

> identified seven themes associated with derailment. Briefly, these themes are: (1) unable to delegate or prioritize; (2) being reactive rather than proactive; (3) unable to maintain relationships with an extended network of contacts; (4) unable to build a team; (5) having poor judgment; (6) being a slow learner; and (7) having an overriding personality defect.[8]

Furnham posits that,

> Executive derailment is *a* function of three things; very-particular personality traits, naive followers and particular situations that create poorly regulated and governed businesses. First, the particular personality traits. Researchers in this area now talk of the "dark triad" of subclinical psychopathy . . . the three interrelated traits of the "dark triad" are arrogance, duplicitousness and emotional coldness. What about the second condition of CEO failure; the naive followers? Some types of people allow derailing leaders to thrive—after all, we get the politicians and leaders we deserve. But there is a type of follower that can be termed "toxic" . . . Toxic followers become particularly dangerous when they sit on the boards of companies with a derailing CEO.[9]

With regard to the third element, Furnham says, "The third component of executive derailment is the social, economic, and legal climate. The toxic leader does best in situations of flux and instability."[10] Furnham also suggests that potential leaders should be screened for "dark side" as well as "bright side" characteristics during the hiring process and lists seven characteristics of leaders with derailment potential,

Arrogance—They are right and everybody else is wrong.
Melodrama—They want to be the center of attention.
Volatility—Their mood swings create business swings.
Excessive caution—They can't make important decisions.
Habitual distrust—They focus on the negatives all the time.
Aloofness—They disengage and disconnect from staff.
Eccentricity—They think it is fun to be different just for the sake of it.
Passive resistance—Their silence is misinterpreted as agreement.
Perfectionism—They get the little things right even if the big things go wrong.
Eagerness to please—They stress that being popular matters most.[11]

BRIGHT SIDE LEADERS

In the discussion of personality characteristics in chapter 7, we touched briefly on the five-factor model (FFM) of personality and shared that the "five factor model rests on the tenet that the attributes of 'extraversion/introversion (or surgency), friendly-ness/hostility (or agreeableness), conscientiousness (or will), neuroticism/emotional stability (or emotional stability), and intellect (or openness)' are the primary factors that determine personality."[12] We also shared that a full review of the FFM model was beyond the scope of that discussion.

Nonetheless, it is important to revisit the five-factor model briefly, as it is generally considered to represent the bright side of personality, and that bright side represents the positive personality attributes of individuals.[13] As Hogan and Kaiser said, "personality predicts leadership—who we are is how we lead."[14] If the positive side, bright side, of a leader's personality is dominant, he/she will tend to act in positive, productive ways. Conversely, if the negative, dark side of his/her personality is dominant, he/she will tend to act in ways that are counterproductive and/or disruptive to organization success.

DARK SIDE LEADERS

As can be seen in the original version of this work in chapter 9, dark side leadership was discussed in some detail; however, an in-depth discussion was not included. In the research done since the publication of the first edition, considerable effort has been expended to better quantify and differentiate dark side from bright side leadership. Two related but different views of dark side leadership emerge from that research.

One view is the principle of "too much of a good thing" (TMGT) effect. According to Pierce and Aquinis, the "TMGT effect occurs when ordinarily beneficial antecedents (i.e., predictor variables) reach inflection points after which their relations with desired outcomes (i.e., criterion variables) cease to be linear and positive."[15] More straightforwardly, Pierce and Aquinis state, "too much of any good thing is ultimately bad."[16] The other view is based on the personality disorders (PDs) listed in the *Diagnostic Manual of Mental Disorders*—5th edition *(DSM-5)*.[17]

The TMGT effect can be seen in numerous areas of organizational leadership. Lusk and Chamorro-Premuzic share that "too much resilience could make people overly tolerant of adversity."[18] Regarding employee engagement, Garrad and Chamorro-Premuzic state that "engagement itself can be a barrier to better performance if it's taken to an extreme."[19]

Xiaotao, Yang, Diaz, and Yu found in a study of inclusive leadership that "task performance increases when inclusive leadership is from low to moderate levels, and task performance decreases when inclusive leadership is from moderate to high levels."[20] Li, Rubenstein, Lin, Wang, and Chen, in a study of leader benevolence, found "when showing too much concern for followers' work and nonwork well-being, they may unintentionally hurt the team by not paying enough attention to structuring team tasks and monitoring team goal pursuit."[21]

A study by Furnham, Treglown, Hyde, and Trickey of leader altruism found a similar result saying that "'Dark' side personality traits which are a manifestation of the personality disorders are also related to the probability of engaging in altruism. And, moreover, that by understanding the personality correlates of the altruistic individual at work it may be possible to identify those most likely to make unethical, immoral or selfish ethical decisions in corporate settings."[22] Even creativity has a dark side related to the TMGT effect.

Chamorro-Premuzic held that "creativity has been associated with a wide range of counterproductive, rarely discussed qualities."[23] He further explains that

> creativity has also been associated with dishonesty, presumably because it enables individuals to creatively distort reality. That is not to say that creative people are necessarily unethical. Rather, their lower tolerance for boredom and conventionality, and their more vivid imaginations, equip them with more sophisticated mental tools to both self-deceive and deceive others.[24]

Gottschall holds that even the emerging power of storytelling in organizations can have a dark side, saying that "like any powerful tool, humans can wield stories for good or ill."[25] Leader charisma can also be debilitating according to Vergauwe, Wille, Hofmans, Kaiser, and De Fruyt who state "our research shows that while having at least a moderate level of charisma is important, having too much may hinder a leader's effectiveness."[26] In summary, keep in mind what Garrad and Chamorro-Premuzic shared, "as the 'too much of a good thing' effect suggests virtually any psychological attribute is problematic at very high levels: e.g., ambition becomes greed, self-esteem becomes narcissism, and creativity turns into odd eccentricity."

Personality disorders as described in *DSM-5* are seen as the counterpoint to the TMGT effect. Dark side leader behavior rather than being based on a leader applying what would otherwise be a positive approach (TMGT) in excess, is based on actual personality disorders. That is not to say that the leader is mentally ill, though in some extreme cases that could be true, but rather that certain aspects of a leader's personality may trend toward being dysfunctional in application.

Miller, Sleep, and Lynam illustrate the relationships.[27] The *DSM-5* domain negative affectivity is associated with the FFM personality trait of neuroticism or emotional stability. Detachment is the *DSM-5* domain associated with FFM low extraversion. Displaying antagonism per *DSM-5* is related to low agreeableness in the FFM model. The *DSM-5* domain of disinhibition has as its counterpart in the FFM low conscientiousness. Psychoticism in the *DSM-5* is associated with high openness. Finally, other facets can come into play such as submissiveness, hostility, perseveration, depressivity, suspiciousness, restricted affectivity, attention seeking, callousness, risk taking, or (lack of) rigid perfectionism.

It is important to note that Miller, Sleep, and Lynam provide specific behaviors related to each *DSM-5* domain and that the typical result for most of the FFM categories is low or in the case of neuroticism (negative affect) and for openness an overabundance of self-revelation.

Other examples of personality disorders can be found in studies related to the aptly named dark triad of Machiavellianism, narcissism, and psychopathy. Page, Bergner, and Wills provide a definition of each of the elements of the dark triad stating that

> Narcissists are characterized by excessive vanity, feelings of superiority and arrogance, as well as a strong need for admiration and entitlement. Think about the type of person who loves to be recognized for an achievement even if they didn't contribute to making it happen. Machiavellians, on the other hand, use manipulative strategies to achieve their goals without considering morality. They are often described as immoral, cynical, and highly calculative; the type of person who thinks that the ends justify the means. Lastly, psychopaths are primarily characterized by high impulsivity, low empathy or interpersonal coldness, as well as by exploitative and antisocial behavior. This type of person is likely to be emotionally charged and unpredictable.[28]

Blair, Helland, and Walton, in a study of narcissism and unethical leadership, found that "as expected, the results of the present study empirically support the relationship between narcissism and a leader's tendency to engage in behaviors associated with unethical leadership."[29] DeShong, Helle, Lengel, Meyer, and Mullins-Sweatt, in a study of the FFM and Machiavellianism, found that "the three Dark Triad (DT) constructs were strongly correlated with all facets of low agreeableness and with the neuroticism facet angry hostility. There was significant overlap in the relationships of psychopathy and Machiavellianism with the FFM facets overall."[30]

A meta-analysis and critical review of the literature on the dark triad led Muris, Merckelbach, Otgaar, and Meijer to state that "narcissists, Machiavellians, and psychopaths often present themselves in a disguised way to other people and tend to wear a mask to hide the darker features of their personality."[31] That finding mirrors the ten-year literature review finding by Furnham, Richards, and Paulhus conducted four years earlier that revealed that each dark triad member "appears to have both adaptive and maladaptive elements."[32]

Whether gauging leader derailment from the TMGT perspective or the personality disorder perspective, it is vital to remember that derailment is not necessarily the end to a leader. All leaders make mistakes and those mistakes can be overcome. Birkinshaw and Haas offer the following three-pronged advice:

> Learn from Every Failure—Begin by getting people to reflect on projects or initiatives that disappointed.

Share the Lessons—While it's useful to reflect on individual failures, the real payoff comes when you spread the lessons across the organization.

Review Your Pattern of Failure—The third step is to take a bird's-eye view of the organization and ask whether your overall approach to failure is working.[33]

Chamorro-Premuzic shared similar advice when he said,

Ask bosses, peers, subordinates, and clients to give you honest and critical feedback on your tendency to display these traits. Tell them that you want to improve and need their candor. How do they see you when you're not at your best? If you identify the traits that trip you up, modify certain behaviors, and continue to adjust in response to critical feedback, you will greatly enhance your reputation, and with it your career and leadership potential.[34]

As Meinert shared, "if leaders are aware of their strengths and weaknesses, they can choose to behave differently."[35] Both Birkinshaw and Haas and Chamorro-Premuzic are suggesting the same strategy we suggest a 360-assessment of an individual's leadership capacity. In doing so, a leader properly exercises his/her leader acumen and avoids derailment.

One last question with the regard to derailment and the most important question is, can derailment be avoided? Van Velsor and Ascalon answer "yes," saying that

Derailment is a fact of life in organizations. Only a relatively few managers will get beyond general management ranks, either because of a lack of fit for more senior level jobs or the lack of open positions in increasingly leaner organizations. Downsizing has added to the likelihood that even generally competent people will derail.

Derailment can be prevented, but only if managers and those around them are willing to work on some relatively tough developmental issues. Improvement in any of the four areas represented by the derailment themes described in this article requires that managers take an in-depth look at personal issues such as self-efficacy, self-esteem, and need for control. Understanding why it may be difficult to relate comfortably to others, to learn in the face of change, or to let go of personal achievement in favor of team-building may involve facing issues around trust, security, self-confidence, or power. The learning that is involved can be highly emotional, demanding an elevated level of readiness or maturity on the part of managers.[36]

George holds that

To stay grounded executives must prepare themselves to confront enormous complexities and pressures. Key concepts include: Leaders who move up have greater freedom to control their destinies, but also experience increased pressure and seduction. Leaders can avoid these pitfalls by devoting themselves to personal development that cultivates their inner compass, or True North. This requires reframing their leadership from being heroes to being servants of the people they lead.[37]

In summary, derailment occurs for a variety of reasons but personality traits such as arrogance or aloofness often play a role while organizational themes such as failure to build a team or to reach established goals may also play a part. George's comments bring us back to the GPS model. Only through developing Leadership Acumen and following an internalized leadership GPS can you navigate through the obstacles you will surely encounter to reach *your True North* and success as a leader.

Chapter 10

The Leadership Journey

So, we've learned all about Leadership Acumen, imprinting, and the leadership GPS model. Now it's time to try out our wheels traveling about the country. Our GPS maps have been updated, we have uploaded our final destination, and we are buckled in ready to make the trip.

The vision for this trip, including the time to start and the estimated time of arrival, are important goals. Yet, there is so much more to the trip. Surely, along the route there will be routine stops for the creature comforts, as well as waypoints as a part of the bigger picture. And, there are always potential hazards along the way in spite of the very best planning.

Automotive imperfections and even possible medical emergencies may lie ahead and temporarily derail even the most prepared driver. However, the most important thing along this journey is to acknowledge the journey itself for *its* value. This trip, regardless of its direction, is part of *your true north*. Within this trip lies a portion of your life and *total* travel time; so be sure to make the most of *all of the journey*, not just arriving at the destination.

Likewise, the whole gamut of leadership is not just about the outcomes, though those are certainly important, but what is equally important is the journey. It's not about when you start or when you finish. Leadership opportunities may come early in a profession while others may come late in a career. Some opportunities may be short-lived while yet others may last an entire career.

Whether the opportunity comes early or late, is short-lived or long-term, the journey is as important as the outcome. It is about what and how you learned and grew along the way. It is about who you help along the way and who helped you (and did you take the time to thank them?). What were the momentous, defining moments in the journey? Did what you have internalized allow you to succeed? Did you enjoy the journey by taking the time to "stop and smell the roses" without getting derailed? When you arrived at your destination, were you able to reflect on the journey and acknowledge highlights, accomplishments, and new awareness?

Bennis described the leadership journey with an analogy to Shakespeare saying that "Shakespeare, who seems to have learned more every time I read him, spoke of the seven ages of man. A leader's life has seven ages as well, and, in many ways, they parallel those Shakespeare describes in *As You Like It*. To paraphrase, these stages can be described as infant, schoolboy, lover, soldier, general, statesman, and sage."[1]

Bennis is referring to a lifetime of leadership. And leadership is just that, a lifetime journey. The transitions Bennis describes will come to all who seek and ultimately fill leadership positions with the passage of time. Aspiring leaders and especially those with the ambition to excel and/or reach the highest leadership levels in their chosen field seldom have time to dwell on the age, the stage, or the transitional period in their early professional years.

Not until they are near the end of their career do they have time to reflect more deeply. That is not to say that leaders do not reflect on what they do, but simply that they often do not reflect regularly on where they are in their career though they should. For only by retrospectively examining what we have said and done, how we have said it or done it, and the outcomes generated by our words and actions, can we truly grow. It is not enough to simply say, "well that worked" or "that did not work."

We must critically examine each step and factor and learn from both our successes and failures. As Polizzi et al. stated, "reflection plays a structural and foundational part in this process of learning from life experiences, and critical self-reflection is a central component to transformative learning."[2] Reflection is also the basis for seeking the learning experiences that will provide continued growth individually and professionally.

For most leaders the transition from one stage to the next is either incremental or comes at such pace as to seem to be seamlessly moving from one leadership role or opportunity to the next. But, most leaders do not see quick jumps from one leadership level to the next. The transitions are typically less rapid calling for longer stops along the way.

As Kotter shared, "the requirements for leadership include some things that are very situation-specific and that tend to take time, often much time, to develop."[3] A select few, through serendipity, good timing, or just "plain old good luck" seem to move through the career stages more rapidly. Kotter observed of these atypical individuals, "all this does not preclude the existence of a few unusually broad and talented people who can move easily across industries and companies. There will always be some people like that. But they will always be rare."[4] Again, we refer back to our reference in chapter 3, of those who are genetically predisposed toward leadership.

The typical leader needs to be a lifelong, reflective learner, one who seeks not only new experiences but experiences related to daily, routine tasks that broaden and deepen his/her leadership skills. Successful leaders are never too old or so experienced that they cannot benefit from learning.

Each of those career changes is like a "leg" of a cross-country trip. Each time you traverse familiar territory, you become more adept at traveling through it and, each time, less in need of your GPS. You learn the pitfalls to avoid and the shortcuts along the route. Mastering the craft and intricacies of leading a business or school takes time and effort. And, school's leaders, though they share some commonalties with their business counterparts, differ in that the product they deal with, educating humans, differs substantially from the typical product of a business enterprise.

Individual people are a lot more variable than components on an assembly line, the branding of a cleaning product, or the dollar balance on a ledger. But whether leading a business or leading a school, a leader needs the skills to manage the interpersonal aspects of the job. He/she needs emotional intelligence and well-developed soft skills.

For some leaders the realization that these skills are needed to be successful at leading a highly diverse cadre of individuals with diverse wants and needs comes early; for others, it comes later. The discerning leader recognizes the need for a skillset to appropriately deal with the human aspect of the job and wisely seeks it out.

This skillset, the five leader imperatives of the Leader GPS Model (credibility, competence, the ability to inspire, vision, and emotional intelligence/soft skills), has been described in the previous chapters. Although having any one of the abilities in the skillset is a plus, none of them individually will create success as a leader. You must at least have a modicum of each of them to be successful, and the more you have, the more likely your success will be. Each skill in the skillset offers its own unique challenges for individual growth and collectively pose an even greater challenge.

The challenge in developing credibility is being consistent. The most blatant departures from consistency (or at least that appearance) often appear in the political arena where candidates argue over the minutiae of the voting records or positions on issues. But that is, after all, politics; positions change, as do votes in favor of or against any given proposition. Politicians often, however, pay a price for confirmed inconsistency. They are voted out.

By analogy the same can be true of all leaders. If a leader fails to live up to the values he/she espouses by being inconsistent; fails to consistently behave ethically and with integrity; shirks responsibility and is not accountable; or, is found to be less than consistently honest, responsible, and sincere, he/she may find that they are turned out or derailed and are unable to lead in their organization. As Baldoni related, it is important that as a leader you should,

"Live your values."[5] For as Baldoni shared about credibility, "Credibility is a leader's coin of the realm. With it, she can lead people to the Promised Land; without it, she wanders in the desert of lost expectations. Once lost it may be impossible to regain, and so the lesson to any manager who has any aspiration of achieving anything is to guard your credibility and take care you never lose it."[6]

But even if a leader can establish credibility through consistently doing what is right, he/she must still exhibit competence to be effective and successful in the long term. Any individual (and especially those who are overly ambitious and/or fail to spend the time in place to master their profession) can find themselves "in over their heads." That is, they may be capable leaders in general, but lack the level of competence required for the position they hold.

Competence, then, is a causal necessity for credibility. You cannot be credible without competence. And, competence requires skills not only in the core, hard skills of a profession but in the soft skill areas related to competence delineated in the leader GPS model: discernibility, perception, conflict resolution skills, problem-solving and decision-making skills, relationship building, planning and implementation, and assessment and evaluation. Lacking "hard core competencies" in any one of these areas will be problematic long term. Skills in these areas must be learned, developed, and continually refined.

If a leader is conscientious in developing and maintaining credibility (and assumes a learning posture that allows him/her to become and remain competent), the probability of being a leader who can inspire others is greatly enhanced. But inspiration, like credibility and competence, must come from a heartfelt genuineness. Those who set out to inspire often find that inspiration is like management of people. Dembowski quotes Quinn as holding that, "People don't often need, or respond well to, being managed."[7]

People must see that a leader displays enthusiasm for what he/she does. That he/she is energetic and passionate. That they are optimistic about current and future events in the organization, courageous in their efforts toward building positive outcomes and genuine in what they say and do. A leader who is credible and competent has the basis for inspiration. But other ingredients also play a part.

To truly inspire, a leader must have a vison for an organization. He/she must also be capable of engaging others in both building and implementing that vision. Engagement of organizational members (and having those same organizational members properly implement the organizational vision) requires those same individuals to believe the leader is committed to the organization and the vison. Additionally, they must believe that he has a true sense of direction for implementing the vision, is professional in his/her handling of people and events, is decisive, constantly works toward realization of the vison, and has an eye in all instances toward success today and tomorrow.

These are skills and dispositions that can be learned and honed over time. They are also skills and dispositions that lend themselves to developing a true followership as a leader, not in the sense of a reverent followership, but of people who believe that you will do *what is right* and do it in the right way because you are about the organization, its members, and the outcomes of the organization.

Emotional intelligence guides the leadership journey of a credible, competent, inspirational leader who has a viable vison that is accepted and acted upon. This is the thread that binds together all of the skills, both hard and soft, and dispositions of the leader. As Goleman shares, emotionally intelligent leaders are self-aware, self-regulating, motivated, display great empathy toward others, and have highly developed social and interpersonal skills.[8] Such leaders have or develop the skills they need and employ them appropriately when called for. They have a broad and inclusive repertoire of knowledge and skills upon which they can draw based on the fact that they are credible, competent, inspirational, visionary, and have the emotional intelligence to navigate the often challenging roads and byways of leadership.

Consummate leaders display skills and dispositions of the leader GPS model. One need only examine the leadership shown by those leaders whose GPS's were fully charged and updated whether by a genetic predisposition or early imprinting (either via stress or desire); the following leaders during their journeys left memorable impressions that will be models for generations of leaders. The charismatic personality and openness of President Ronald Wilson Reagan; the tenacity and genuineness of the Reverend Billy Graham; the relentless and enthusiastic nature of Coach Pat Summit; the tireless compassion of Martin Luther King, Junior, and the idealism and energy of Steve Jobs—all leaders in different ways, yet all possessing the skillset to have had hundreds of thousands of willing and enthusiastic followers, even today.

In closing, we return to Nancy Koehn's *Leadership Journey of Abraham Lincoln*. In the book, she points out the critical experiences and characteristics Lincoln endured and developed as he journeyed to the presidency and leadership of the United States in the most troubled time of our nation. Among those experiences and characteristics were discernment, disappointment, triumph and tragedy, loneliness, Gettysburg, transformational change, and the exercise of willpower. Of discernment, the lesson learned from Lincoln according to Koehn was that the ability to focus on critical issues is vital to success.[9] As Koehn shared,

> Leaders trying to accomplish a worthy mission have to cultivate the ability to identify the one, two, or three essential issues facing them at a given moment. It is never five or ten. It is always one or two—maybe three—issues that really matter. Having identified these, leaders must let the remaining concerns go,

either by giving themselves permission to turn their attention away from all that is not central to their purpose or by handing peripheral issues to others, including an adversary. Being able to do this—to concentrate on the most important issues while relinquishing the rest—depends on a leader's willingness to recognize two things: first, he or she cannot do it all, and second, by saying no to that which is not mission critical, one is actually saying yes to that which is.[10]

Disappointment was also a useful experience for Lincoln according to Koehn. As she shared, "The making of courageous leaders is rarely swift and smooth. Indeed, the setbacks and the times that Lincoln spent *not* being able to gratify his ambitions were important ingredients in the wisdom, resilience, and empathy that he nurtured and then used so successfully."[11] The important lesson is that a leader will not always be successful. Errors and missteps will be made. Success comes to those who preserve and overcome setbacks.

That willingness to persevere will lead to diverse outcomes, as it did for Lincoln who experienced both triumph and tragedy. Lincoln was elected president, a personal triumph that eventually led to Civil War, a decidedly personal and national tragedy. The most erudite leader will experience unanticipated results that taint triumph with, if not tragedy, disappointment.

Fully realizing the weight of decisions a leader must make and that those decisions are for the leader and the leader alone, no matter what advice or counsel he/she receives, is another lesson from Lincoln. All other considerations aside, if catastrophe occurs, the leader is ultimately responsible. He or she is alone at the top, a lonely place in those instances.

Gettysburg was a pivotal moment in the Civil War and also a pivotal moment for Lincoln in reinforcing the need to devote every energy to accomplishing the mission (saving the union and ending slavery) the battle exemplified. As Koehn shared, "we can take from his leadership the critical importance of framing the stakes of a particular moment. This means connecting current change efforts to the history and future of the enterprise, locating these efforts in the arc of ongoing events, explaining each stakeholder's role in the process, identifying the specific trade-offs of making the change, and understanding these costs in relation to the ultimate goal."[12] Staying focused and on-task when the cost is high (organizational success and therefore personal success) is a crucial to successful leadership.

The issue for Lincoln, before and after Gettysburg, and the issue for all leaders is change. For Lincoln, the change was transforming the nation. Transformational change for 21st century organizational leaders fails to reach that level of challenge but is nonetheless just as vital to organizational survival. Managing change successfully is a basal component of leader success.

A final point of emphasis in Koehn's book is the exertion of willpower.[13] Lincoln was so tired by the miseries of war and the restlessness of a war weary nation that he considered what had been an unacceptable alternative—a negotiated peace. His power of will, however, allowed him to maintain his belief in the rightness of his actions and the eventual positive outcome, albeit with horrendous sacrifice of lives. The lesson for leaders is clear—stay the course when you are right.

Koehn ends her narrative by saying that "Lincoln's journey was one of learning by doing, ongoing commitment to bettering himself, keen intelligence harnessed to equally acute emotional awareness, and the moral seriousness into which he grew as he attained immense power."[14] It was also an all-too-human path marked by setbacks, derailments, and disappointments. It is a path familiar to all leaders. Nothing comes easily or without difficulty. If the end is worthy, difficulties can be overcome to reach a positive outcome. That positive outcome can be reached more easily by developing and using your leader acumen.

Notes

INTRODUCTION

1. Jim Kouzes and Barry Posner, *The Truth about Leadership—The No-fads, to the Heart-of-the-Matter Facts You Need to Know* (Hoboken, NJ: Wiley & Sons, Inc., 2010).
2. Tom Rath and Barry Conchie, *Strengths-Based Leadership* (New York, NY: Gallup Press, 2008).
3. Nancy Koehn, "The Leadership Journey of Abraham Lincoln." *Mckinsey Quarterly, (2)*, 77–87, (2018).
4. Wanda S. Maulding Green and Edward E. Leonard, *Leadership Intelligence: Navigating to Your True North,* p. 3 (2016).
5. Koehn, "The Leadership Journey of Abraham Lincoln."
6. Scott Gregory, "The Most Common Type of Incompetent Leader." *Harvard Business Review Digital Articles*, 2–4 (2018).

CHAPTER 1

1. Benjamen Bloom, "New Views of the Learner: Implications for Instruction and Curriculum." *Educational Leadership* (1978) 563–579.
2. Daniel Goleman, "What Makes a Leader?" In *On Emotional Intelligence.* Harvard Business Review (Boston, MA: Harvard Review Press, 2015), 7.
3. Daniel Goleman, Richard Boyatzis, and Annie McKee. *Primal Leadership* (Boston, MA: Harvard Business Press, 2010).
4. GMAC.com/market-intelligence-and-research/research-library/curriculum-insight/2014-gmegs-survey-report.aspx
5. Bloom, "New Views of the Learner."
6. Howard Gardner, *Frames of Mind: The Theory of Multiple Intelligences* (New York, NY: Basic Books, 1983).

7. Klaus Immelmann. "Ecological Significance of Imprinting and Early Learning," *Annual Review of Ecology and Systematics*, 6 (1975) 15–37.

8. Branti Film Productions (Producers). Carroll Ballard (Director). *Fly Away Home*. United States, Columbia Pictures (1996).

9. Bill Lishman. *Father Goose*. Toronto: Little, Brown Canada. (1995).

10. Robert Miller. *Imprint Training of the Newborn Foal*. Augusta, GA: Morris Communications Corporation (2003).

11. Christopher Marquis and Andras Tilscik. "Imprinting: Toward a Multilevel Theory." *Academy of Management Annals*. New York: Routledge (2013).

12. Ibid.

13. Arthur Stinchcombe. "Social Structure and Organizations." In J. G. March, *Handbook of Organizations*. Chicago, IL: Rand McNally (1965).

14. Pete Hall. "Building Bridges: Strengthening the Principal Induction Process through Intentional Mentoring." *Phi Delta Kappan*, 89(6) (2008) 449–452.

15. James Kouzes and Barry Posner. "Challenge Is the Opportunity for Greatness." *Leader to Leader*. (28) (2003) 16–23.

16. Christopher Marquis and Andras Tilcsik. "Imprinting: Toward a Multi-Level Theory." *The Academy of Management Annals*, 7(1) (2013) 195–245.

17. Ibid.

18. Monica Higgins. *Career Imprints: Creating Leaders across an Industry* (1st edition), San Francisco, CA; Jossey-Bass (2005).

19. Marquis and Tilscik. *Imprinting: Toward a Multilevel Theory*.

20. Zeki Simsek, Brian Fox, and Ciaran Heavey. "What's Past Is Prologue: Framework, Review, and Future Directions for Organizational Research on Imprinting." *Journal of Management*. 41 (1) (January 2015) 288–317.

21. Ibid.

22. Together, the framework suggests that the conceptual domain of imprinting can be organized around five core constructs: *the imprinters, the imprinted*, and the *imprinting processes* that collectively constitute the genesis of imprints, the subsequent evolutionary *dynamics* (path, duration, and evolution of imprints) that contribute to the metamorphosis of imprints, and the *impact of imprints* that become manifest to varying degrees in various outcomes (the outcomes and implications that follow from imprints). Interrelating these constructs, the framework emphasizes fundamental distinctions in the formation, development or dynamics, and consequences of imprinting. We would, however, hasten to add that there are likely interdependencies and interactions across the phases. Interdependencies occur because the process by which imprints form may shape the subsequent evolution of imprints. Similarly, the nature and evolution of imprints affect the magnitude, timing, and direction of their outcomes. Interactions may also occur between imprinting sources, processes, and dynamics across micro and macro levels of analysis (Marquis & Tilcsik, 2013; Simsek 2015).

23. He goes onto suggest that "that imprinting involves three processes in which an imprint is formed (*genesis*), evolves and morphs (*metamorphosis*), and eventually becomes manifest in outcomes (*manifestations*)." He expands those concepts in relating that imprinting involves "*imprinters, imprinted, imprinting,*

imprint dynamics, and *impact of imprints*" (Semsik 2015). The key underlying mechanism is that, during periods of organizational and professional socialization, "individuals are particularly susceptible to influence . . . because of the great uncertainty regarding role requirements" (Ashforth and Saks, 1996: 149). Because individuals are highly motivated to reduce such uncertainty, they become especially receptive to cues from the environment (Schein, 1971). Thus, the first exposure to the practical aspects of a job or position is often highly formative. With limited prior experience in the position, people are not only more open to learning new skills but also "more receptive to learning . . . work routines and practices" (Briscoe and Kellogg, 2011: 295). Later, by contrast, people tend to be "less receptive to learning and, therefore, are not susceptible to imprinting" (McEvily, Jaffee, and Tortoriello, 2012: 552).

24. Marquis and Tilcsik. *Imprinting: Toward a Multi-Level Theory.*
25. Prahbir Jha, "Build Your Career with Teamwork, Diverse Skills." *The Times of India* (November 8, 2017).
26. Ibid.
27. Sydney Finkelstein, "The Best Leaders Are Great Teachers." *Harvard Business Review*, 96(1) (2018) 142–145.
28. Dobrev Stanislav & Merluzzi, Jennifer, "Stayers versus Movers: Social Capital and Early Career Imprinting among Young Professionals." *Journal of Organizational Behavior*, 39(1) (2016) 67–81. doi:10.1002/job.2210.
29. Karen Christensen, "'Imprinting' in the Workplace." *Rotman Management* (2015) 108–110.
30. Uzzi, B., Yang Yang, and K. Gaughan. 2016. "The Formation and Imprinting of Network Effects among the Business Elite [ArXiv]." ArXiv, June. doi:1606.02283.
31. Linda Tyler, "Imprinting Leadership." *American Journal of Health-System Pharmacy*, 73(17) (2016) 1339–1346. doi:10.2146/ajhp150991.
32. Gloria Crisp and Kelly Alvarado-Young, "The Role of Mentoring in Leadership Development." *New Directions for Student Leadership*, 158 (2018) 37–47.
33. Jason Lortie, *Imprinting effects of Founding Conditions, Structure, and Capabilities on Social and Financial Organizational Outcome Satisfaction* (2016, Order No. 10300355).
34. Stephen Lippmann and Howard Aldrich, "A Rolling Stone Gathers Momentum: Generational Units, Collective Memory, and Entrepreneurship." *Academy of Management Review*, 41(4) (2016) 658–675. doi:10.5465/amr.2014.0139
35. Shmuel Ellis, Barak Aharonson, Isreal Drori, & Zur Shapira, "Imprinting through Inheritance: A Multi-Genealogical Study of Entrepreneurial Proclivity." *Academy of Management Journal*, 60(2) (2017) 500–522. doi:10.5465/amj.2014.0150
36. Jim Kouzes and Barry Posner, "Who You Are Isn't Who You Will Be." *Leader to Leader*, 83 (2017) 30–34. doi:10.1002/ltl.20273
37. Ibid.
38. Ibid.
39. Craig Pearce and Charles Manz, "The Leadership Disease . . . and Its Potential Cures." *Business Horizons*, 57(2) (2014) 215–224. doi:10.1016/j.bushor.2013.11.005

40. Stephen Brookfield, *Powerful Techniques for Teaching Adults*. San Francisco, CA: Jossey-Bass, a Wiley Imprint, 2013.

41. Cody Cox, Laura Barron, William Davis, and Bernardo de la Garza, "Using Situational Judgment Tests (SJTs) in Training: Development and Evaluation of a Structured, Low-fidelity Scenario-based Training Method." *Personnel Review*, 46(1) (2017) 36–45. doi 10.1108/PR-05-2015-0137.

42. Peter Sørensen, "What Research on Learning Transfer Can Teach about Improving the Impact of Leadership-Development Initiatives?" *Consulting Psychology Journal: Practice and Research*, 69(1) (2017) 47–62. http://dx.doi.org/10.1037/cpb0000072.

43. Ibid.

44. David Ulrich and Norm Smallwood, "Building a Leadership Brand." *Harvard Business Review*, 85(7–8) (2007) 92.

45. Ibid.

46. Council of Chief State School Officers (2018). PSEL 2015 and Promoting Principal Leadership for the Success of Students with Disabilities. Retrieved from https://ccsso.org/sites/default/files/2017-11/PSELforSWDs01252017.pdf

47. Alissa Harrison, Millennial Leadership Development: Building Competencies with Best Practices (2015, Order No. 10042184). Available from ProQuest Dissertations & Theses Global. (1775507227).

48. Ibid.

49. Marcus Buckingham, "Leadership Development in the Age of the Algorithm." *Harvard Business Review*, 90(6) (2012) 86.

50. Umair Haque, "Making Room for Reflection Is a Strategic Imperative." Retrieved from https://hbr.org/2010/11/reflection-items-not-action-it?

51. Ibid.

52. Jennifer Porter, "Why You Should Make Time for Self-Reflection (Even If You Hate Doing It)." *Harvard Business Review Digital Articles*, 2–4 (2017).

53. Martin Reeves, Roselinde Torres, and Fabien. Hassan, "How to Regain the Lost Art of Reflection." *Harvard Business Review Digital Articles*, (2017) 2–6.

54. Catherin Bailey & Adrain Madden *MIT Sloan Management Review* 57, no. 4 (Summer 2016) 53–61. 62.

55. Kouzes and Posner, 2017.

CHAPTER 2

1. Christopher Marquis and Andras Tilcsik. "Imprinting: Toward a Multi-Level Theory." *The Academy of Management Annals*, 7 (1). (2013) 195–245.

2. Joseph Luft and Harry Ingham, "The Johari Window." *Human Relations Training News*, 5(1), (1961) 6–7.

3. Amy Jen Su and Muril Wilkins. (2013). To Strengthen Your Confidence, Look to Your Past. Retrieved from https://hbr.org/2013/04/to-strengthen-your-confidence

4. George Hollenbeck and Douglas Hall, "Self-Confidence and Leader Performance." *Organizational Dynamics*, 33(3) (2004) 254–269.

5. Alexander Stajkovic and Fred Luthans, "Self-Efficacy and Work-Related Performance: A Meta-Analysis." *Psychological Bulletin*, 124(2) (1998) 240–261. doi:10.1037/0033-2909.124.2.240

6. Albert Bandura, "Insights. Self-efficacy." *Harvard Mental Health Letter*, 13(9) (1997) 4–6.

7. Bandura, Albert. 1993. "Perceived Self-Efficacy in Cognitive Development and Functioning." *Educational Psychologist* 28 (2): 117. doi:10.1207/s15326985ep2802_3.

8. Rebecca Knight, "How to Prove Yourself after a Promotion." *Harvard Business Review Digital Articles* (2018) 2–6.

9. Jim Dillon. (2017). "Leading with Humility." *Educational Leadership*. https://www.smartbrief.com/original/2017/07/leading-humility.

10. Margarita Mayo, "If Humble People Make the Best Leaders, Why Do We Fall for Charismatic Narcissists?" Retrieved from https://hbr.org/2017/04/if-humble-people-make-the-best-leaders-why-do-we-fall-for-charismatic-narcissists

11. Dan Cable, "How Humble Leadership Really Works." *Harvard Business Review Digital Articles* (2018) 2–5.

12. Jia Hu, Berrin Erdogan, Jiang Kaifeng, and Talya Bauer, "Research: When Being a Humble Leader Backfires." *Harvard Business Review Digital Articles* (2018) 1–5.

13. Kayla Walters and Dalia Diab, "Humble Leadership: Implications for Psychological Safety and Follower Engagement." *Journal of Leadership Studies*, 10(2) (2016) 7–18. doi:10.1002/jls.21434

14. Merwyn Hayes, Michael Comer, "Lead with Humility." *Leadership Excellence Essentials*, 28(9) (2011) 13.

15. Linda Ruffenach, "Unicorns, Leprechauns & the Complete Leader: Why Humility Is Important in Leadership." *Leadership Excellence Essentials*, 34(7) (2017) 10–11.

CHAPTER 3

1. Cracking the dress code dilemma. Salaryforbusiness.com, http://business.salary.com/cracking-the-dress-code-dilemma/ (2015).

2. Lou Solomon. "The Top Complaints from Employees about Their Leaders." *Harvard Business Review, NY*. Retrieved from: https://hbr.org/2015/06/the-top-complaints-from-employees-about-their-Leaders.

3. James Kouzes and Barry Pozner. *Credibility: How Leaders Gain and Lose It, Why People Demand It.* San Francisco, CA: Jossey-Bass (2011).

4. Brian Leavy. "Understanding the Triad of Great Leadership—Context, Conviction, and Credibility." *Strategy and Leadership*. 31(1), 56.

5. Brenda DePuy. "The Linchpins of Leadership." *Public Manager*. 44(2) (2015) 6–8.

6. Stephen R. Covey. "Unifying Leadership." *Executive Excellence*. 16(10) (1999) 3.

7. Ken Blanchard, *The Secret: What Great Leaders Know and Do*. San Francisco, CA: Berrett-Koeher Publishers, Inc. (2001).

8. https://en.wikipedia.org/wiki/Walter_Cronkite.

9. Prasad Kaipi. (2012). "Recover Your Credibility." Retrieved from https://hbr.org/2012/07/recover-your-credibility.

10. DePuy, "The Linchpins of Leadership."

11. Jim Kouzes. *T + D.* 64(9) (2010) 70–71.

12. Bob Pockrass. *Sporting News,* May 5, 2014, http://www.sportingnews.com/nascar-news/4582977-dale-earnhardt-jr-strategy-talladega-finish-results-fan-reaction-tweets/

13. Angie Morgan, "The 4 Keys to Credibility." *Chief Learning Officer, 16*(8), 66, 2017.

14. Ralph Williams, Deana Raffo, and Leigh Anne Clark, "Charisma as an Attribute of Transformational Leaders: What about Credibility?" *Journal of Management Development,* 37(6) (2018) 512–524. doi:10.1108/JMD-03-2018-0088.

15. Neeraj Jaiswal and Rajib Dhar, "The Influence of Servant Leadership, Trust in Leader and Thriving on Employee Creativity." *Leadership & Organizational Development Journal,* 38(1) (2015) 2–21. doi: 10.1108/LODJ-02-2015-0017.

16. Daniel Han Ming Chng, Tae-Yeol Kim, Brad Gilbreath, and Lynne Andersson, "Why People Believe in Their Leaders—or Not." *MIT Sloan Management Review,* 60(1) (2018) 65–70.

17. Krisztina Timko, "Men and Women Are Equally Effective," Munich Personal RePEc Archive. Online at https://mpra.ub.uni-muenchen.de/77022/ Paper No. 77022, posted 2 March 2017 16:07 UTC.

18. Ani Yuningsih and Dadan Mulyana, "Communication Pattern and Skill of Leader in Private University Management." MIMBAR, 33(1) (June 2017) 166–173.

19. Amos Engelbrecht, Gardielle Heine, and Bright Mahembe, "Integrity, Ethical Leadership, Trust and Work Engagement." *Leadership & Organization Development Journal,* 38(3) (2017) 368–379.

20. Patrycia Gulak-Lipka, "The Role of Trust for Leadership in Team." *Sports Journal of Corporate Responsibility and Leadership.* 3(3) (2016). doi: http://dx.doi.org/10.12775/JCRL.2016.015

21. A. Petty, "How to Build Credibility as a Manager." *Government Executive,* 1, 2018.

22. Jim Bracchitta, "Getting It Right the First Time." *Benefits Magazine,* 53(7) (2016) 40.

23. Aren Langvardt. "Ethical Leadership and the Dual Roles of Examples." In *CIBERSpecial Issue: Business Ethics & Intellectual Property in the Global Marketplace* (2012).

24. James Kouzes and Barry Posner. "To Lead, Create a Shared Vision." *Harvard Business Review.* 87(1) (2009) 20–21.

25. Galindo, "The Power of Accountability."

26. Ibid.

27. Warren Bennis. *On Becoming a Leader.*

28. Carly Fiorina. *Tough Choices: A Memoir.* New York: Portfolio (2006).

CHAPTER 4

1. Giles, Sunnie. 2016. "The Most Important Leadership Competencies, According to Leaders Around the World." *Harvard Business Review Digital Articles*, March, 2–6. http://search.ebscohost.com.lynx.lib.usm.edu/login.aspx?direct=true&db=bth&AN=118706315&site=ehost-live.
2. Ibid, p.2.
3. Ibid.
4. Agnieszka Postuła, and Julita Majczyk, "Managers and Leaders in Need of Entrepreneurial Competences." *Entrepreneurial Business & Economics Review*, 6(1) (2018) 97. doi:10.15678/EBER.2018.060105.
5. Ibid.
6. Ineta Portnova and Liga Peiseniece, "Leaders' Competences for Successful Leadership of Invention and Implementation of Innovation: A Conceptual Model." *Journal of Business Management*, (13) (2017) 40–55.
7. Jan Porvaznik, Ivana Ljudvigova, and Anrdea Čajková, "Holistic Competence of Leadership and Managerial Subjects." *Political Sciences / Politické Vedy*, 21(2) (2018) 56–77. doi:10.24040/politickevedy.2018.21.2.56–77
8. Ibid.
9. Kerri Heath, Lene Martin, and Linda Shahisaman, "Global Leadership Competence: The Intelligence Quotient of a Modern Leader." *Journal of Leadership Education*, 16(3) (2017) 134–145.
10. Mrgha Gupta, and Kanika Bhal, "LMX & Leader Competence: Impact on Subordinates' Perceived Cohesion." *Indian Journal of Industrial Relations*, 53(2) (2017) 277–289.
11. Wanda S. Maulding Green and Edward E. Leonard, *Leadership Intelligence: Navigating to Your True North*, 1st edition. Lanham, MD: Rowman & Littlefield, p. 37 (2016).
12. Ineta Portnova and Lega Peiseniece, p. 48.
13. Nguyen Minh, Yuosre Badir, Nguyen Quang, Bilal Afsar, "The Impact of Leaders' Technical Competence on Employees' Innovation and Learning." *Journal of Engineering & Technology Management*, 44 (2017) 44–57. doi:10.1016/j.jengtecman.2017.03.003.
14. Benjamin Artz, Amanda Goodall, and Andrew Oswald, "Boss Competence and Worker Well-Being."
15. Ning Wang, Stephen Wilhite, and Daniel Martino, "Understanding the Relationship between School Leaders' Social and Emotional Competence and Their Transformational Leadership: The Importance of Self-Other Agreement." *Educational Management Administration & Leadership*, 44(3) (2016) 467–490.
16. Rachel Sturm, Dusya Vera, and Mary Crossan, "The Entanglement of Leader Character and Leader Competence and Its Impact on Performance." *The Leadership Quarterly*, 28(3), (2017) 349–366. doi:10.1016/j.leaqua.2016.
17. Ibid.
18. Dora Capozza, Andrea Bobbio, Gian Di Bernardo, Rossella Falvo, and Ariela Pagani, "Leaders' Competence and Warmth: Their Relationships with Employees' Well-Being and Organizational Effectiveness." *TPM-Testing, Psychometrics, Methodology in Applied Psychology*, 24(2) (2017) 185–214.

19. Jennifer Klatt, Sabrina Eimler, and Nicole Krämer, "Makeup Your Mind: The Impact of Styling on Perceived Competence and Warmth of Female Leaders." *Journal of Social Psychology*, 156(5) (2016) 483–497.

20. Rebecca Knight, "How to Prove Yourself after a Promotion." *Harvard Business Review Digital Articles* (2018) 2–6.

21. Byun Gukdo, Ye Dai, Soojin Lee, Seungwan Kang, "Leader Trust, Competence, LMX, and Member Performance: A Moderated Mediation Framework. *Psychological Reports*, 120(6) (2017) 1137–1159. doi:10.1177/0033294117716465

22. Katrien Fransen, Maarten Vansteenkiste, Gert Vande Broek, and Filip Boen, "The Competence-Supportive and Competence-Thwarting Role of Athlete Leaders: An Experimental Test in a Soccer Context." *PLoS ONE* 13(7) (2018) 1–21. doi:10.1371/journal.pone.0200480.

23. Lee G. Bolman, and Terrance E. Deal. *Reframing Organizations: Artistry, Choice, and Leadership*. 4th edition. San Francisco, CA: Jossey-Bass (2015).

24. Christopher Day and David Gurr. *Leading Schools Successfully: Stories from the Field*. London: Routledge (2014), pp. 194–208.

25. Bolman and Deal, *Reframing Organizations: Artistry, Choice and Leadership*.

26. Ibid.

27. Reina, Dennis S., and Michelle L. Reina. 1999. *Trust & Betrayal in the Workplace: Building Effective Relationships in Your Organization*. San Francisco: Berrett-Koehler Publishers.

CHAPTER 5

1. United States Department of Defense. *GPS Spectrum and Interference Issues*. Retrieved from: http://www.gps.gov/spectrum/ 2012.

2. John Baldoni. "Use Your Leadership Presence to Inspire." *Harvard Business Review*, https://hbr.org/2010/05/use-your-leadership-presence-to-inspire, 2010.

3. Peter F. Drucker. "What Makes an Effective Executive?" *Harvard Business Review*. 82(6) (2004) 58–63.

4. Baldoni. "Use Your Leadership Presence to Inspire."

5. http://www.thefamouspeople.com/profiles/martin-luther-king-jr-48.php

6. John Baldoni. "Wanted: Inspirational Leaders." *Conference Board Review*. 46(4) (2009) 6–7.

7. Meena Wilson and Susan Rice. "Wired to Inspire: Leading Organizations through Adversity." *Leadership in Action*, 24(2) (May 2004) 3–7.

8. Dov Seidman. "Catalyzing Inspirational Leadership: Approaches and Metrics for Twenty-First-Century Executives." *Leader to Leader*. 2(68) (2013) 33–40.

9. Eric Garton, and Michael Mankins. "Engaging Your Employees Is Good, but Don't Stop There." *Harvard Business Review Digital Articles*, 2–6 (2015) 3.

10. Ibid.

11. Dembowski, Frederick. 2006. "The Changing Roles of Leadership and Management in Educational Administration." *International Journal of Educational Leadership Preparation* 1(1). http://search.ebscohost.com.lynx.lib.usm.edu/login.aspx?direct=true&db=eric&AN=EJ1066775&site=ehost-live.

12. Midhelle Bligh, and Gregory Hess, "The Power of Leading Subtly: Alan Greenspan, Rhetorical Leadership, and Monetary Policy." *The Leadership Quarterly*, 18(2) (2007) 87–104.

13. Jasmine Vergauwe, Bart Wille, Joeri Hofmans, Robert Kaiser, and Filip De Fruyt, "Too Much Charisma Can Make Leaders Look Less Effective." *Harvard Business Review Digital Articles*, 2–6 (2017).

14. Jon Maner, "Good Bosses Switch between Two Leadership Styles." *Harvard Business Review Digital Articles*, 2–5 (2016) 3.

15. Nick Morgan, "Understand the 4 Components of Influence." *Harvard Business Review Digital Articles*, 2–4 (2015) 3.

16. Emma Seppala, "To Motivate Employees, Do 3 Things Well." *Harvard Business Review Digital Articles*, 2–4 (2016).

17. Ibid.

18. Nathan Washburn and Benjamin Galvin. "Make Sure Your Employees Have Good Things to Say about You Behind Your Back." *Harvard Business Review Digital Articles*, 2–5 (2016).

19. Ibid.

20. Carmine Gallo. "Inspiring Storytellers Transform Employees into Crusaders." *Leader to Leader* 82 (2016) 35–39. doi:10.1002/ltl.20259

21. Dov Seidman and Clifton Leaf, "The Four Pillars of Moral Leadership." *Fortune*, 176(4) (2017) 90–92.

22. Jack Zenger and Joseph Folkman, "The Traits of Leaders Who Do Things Fast and Well." *Harvard Business Review Digital Articles* (2016) 2–4.

23. Nick Tasler, "You Don't Need Charisma to Be an Inspiring Leader." *Harvard Business Review Digital Articles* (2015) 2–4.

24. Katrian Fransen, Niklas Steffens, Alexander Haslam, Norbert Vanbeselaere, Gert Vande Broek, and Filip Boen. "We Will Be Champions: Leaders' Confidence in 'Us' Inspires Team Members' Team Confidence and Performance." *Scandinavian Journal of Medicine & Science in Sports* 26(12) (December 2016) 1455–1469.

25. Kristi Hedges, "How to Rediscover Your Inspiration at Work." *Harvard Business Review Digital Articles*, 1–4 (2017).

26. Lori Hoffner, "Leadership Is More Than a Noun." *Parks & Recreation*, 53(5) (2018) 50.

27. Jacob Heller, David Notgrass, and Charlene Conner, "Moderators to the Relationship between Leaders' Inspirational Behaviors and Followers' Extra Effort." *International Journal of Business and Public Administration (IJBPA)* 1 (2017) 36.

28. Michael Beck, "From Leader to an Inspiring Leader." *Leadership Excellence Essentials*, 33(2) (2016) 40.

29. Eric Garton, "How to Be an Inspiring Leader." *Harvard Business School Cases*, 1 (2017).

30. Andy Bird, "The Alchemy of Leadership Inspiration." *Market Leader*, Q1 (January 2018) 28–31.

31. Jack Zenger and Joseph Folkman. "I'm the Boss! Why Should I Care If You Like Me?" Retrieved from https://hbr.org/2013/05/im-the-boss-why-should-i-care.

32. Jerry L. Patterson and Paul Kelleher. *Resilient School Leaders: Strategies for Turning Adversity into Achievement*, Association for Supervision & Curriculum Development (ASCD). Alexandria, VA: ASCD (2005).

33. Alaina Love. "Leadership, Passion, and the Presidency." *Harvard Business Review*. Retrieved from https://hbr.org/2008/10/leadership-passion-and-the-presidency/ (2008).

34. Donovan MacFarlane. "Impressed and Inspired: Encountering Genuine Leadership with Dr. Barry Posner and Dr. Agueda Ogazon." *E Journal of Organizational Learning & Leadership*, 9(1) (2011) 26–48.

CHAPTER 6

1. Burt Nanus. "Leading the Vision Team." *The Futurist*, 30(3) (1996) 20.

2. James Collins and Jerry Porras. "Building Your Company's Vision." *Harvard Business Review* 74(5) (1996) 65–77.

3. Ibid.

4. Warren Bennis. "The Seven Ages of the Leader." *Harvard Business Review* 82(1) (2004) 46–53.

5. Ibid.

6. Ibid.

7. James Kouzes and Barry Posner. "To Lead, Create a Shared Vision." *Harvard Business Review* 87(1) (2009) 20–21.

8. John Kotter. "What Leaders Really Do?" *Harvard Business Review*. 68(3) (1990) 103–111.

9. Ibid.

10. Ibid.

11. Daniel Goleman. "Leading for the Long Future." *Leader to Leader*. 2014(72) (2014) 34–39.

12. Ibid.

13. Stephen Covey. "Four Traits of Great Leaders." *Leadership Excellence Essentials*. 22(11) (2005) 4–5.

14. Kouzes and Posner. "To Lead, Create a Shared Vision."

15. Ibid.

16. Burt Nanus. *Visionary leadership: Creating a Compelling Sense of Direction for Your Organization*. San Francisco, CA: Jossey-Bass (1992).

17. Joseph Murphy and Daniela Torre. "Vision: Essential Scaffolding." *Educational Management Administration & Leadership*. 43(2) (2015) 177–197.

18. Sylvia Méndez-Morse. "Vision, Leadership, and Change." SEDL. *Issues . . . about Change* 2(3) (1993). Retrieved from: http://www.sedl.org/change/issues/issues23.html (1993).

19. Ibid.

20. There are various approaches that have been suggested for the actual development of a shared vision that then is expressed in a vision statement (Blokker, 1989; Nanus, 1992; Rogus, 1990). Educators will undoubtedly adjust the steps listed below

to their unique situation since there is a different focus when applying the steps at the district or school level. Four steps facilitate the conceptualization of vision and lead to it becoming a vision statement. **1. Know your organization.** During the initial phase of formulating a vision, it is important to learn everything about the organization as it currently exists. This corresponds to Manasse's concept of organizational vision, "a comprehensive picture of the existing system within its environment." She suggests that organizational vision involves a system's perspective to determine the components of a school or district and how they are interrelated. Boyd (1992b) provides a comprehensive list of contextual factors that influence the change process which can serve as a guide to knowing a school or district. It is important that a school leader understand the important role of a school's ecology—the physical and material aspects such as school size—and a school's culture—the attitudes and beliefs, norms, and relationships. Nanus (1992) suggests that "the basic nature" of an organization can be defined by determining its present purpose and its value to society. Knowing what a school or district is about and the reason for its existence is the first step in developing a vision statement. Knowing the collective understanding of an organization is the second step and includes the participation of constituencies. **2. Involve critical individuals.** The individuals or groups identified as constituencies include those that are the most critical, both inside and outside, to a school or district. These "critical" individuals can be those who are essential, such as a representative of a major business in the community and those people who tend to judge severely, such as the consistently vocal parent. Consider the major expectations or interests of these critical constituents as well as any threats or opportunities that may originate from these groups or individuals. Educators should involve individuals such as students, parents, business leaders, and other community members. They should also ensure the participation of children advocacy groups that work with their students and major employers of their students, as well as representatives of post-secondary institutions that serve their students. The involvement of critical individuals often presents challenges to the development of a shared vision. Rogus (1990) suggests having the participants write their ideas before a meeting; identify consensus statements first and then grapple with nonconsensus statements at the meeting. Remember that consensus is the absence of serious disagreement, not total agreement with everything. Aside from describing the organization and discussing its purpose, the group participates in discussing the factors that could impact the school or district. **3. Explore the possibilities.** In her definition of future vision, Manasse (1986) advocates considering future developments and trends that may influence a school or district. Possible major changes in the economical, social, political, and technological arenas that will impact a school or district should be explored. Specific questions that educators should consider are: (a) *What are possible future trends of students' needs?* (b) *What are possible future trends in parents' needs or requirements that will impact our students?* (c) *What are possible future expectations or requirements of our students from employers or post-secondary institutions?* (d) *What possible changes in social, economic, political, or technical areas will impact our organization?* The exploration of possible futures can be encouraged with the provision of literature concerning future trends. Another strategy that can assist participants to speculate about the future is to view and discuss videotapes that have been produced by futurists. **4. Put it in writing.** The final step is writing a clear and concise vision statement. This step uses all the information gathered and discussed, the descriptions of the school or district, as well as the predictions of future developments and trends that will impact a school or district. It flows from the discussion of the most probable future of the school or district. Rogus (1990) suggests using the consensus statements to begin writing the vision statement, getting one "last set of reactions," and having the total faculty determine its final form. This final step is the result of much discussion by the people involved and aside from "distilling" the issues discussed, it focuses the group's attention to what they agreed upon and their united vision for their school or district. This vision then is committed to paper.

21. Wanda S. Maulding Green and Edward E. Leonard. *Leadership Intelligence: Navigating to Your True North*, 1st ed. Lanham, MD: Rowman & Littlefield (2016).

22. Ron Ashkenas and Brook Manville, "The Six Fundamental Skills Every Leader Should Practice." *Harvard Business Review Digital Articles*, 1–4 (2018).

23. Robert Quinn and Anjan Thakor, Creating a Purpose-Driven Organization. (cover story). *Harvard Business Review,* 96(4) (2018) 78–85.

24. Ibid.

25. John Baur, Parker Ellen, Ronald Buckley, Gerald Ferris, Thomas Allison, Aaron McKenny, and Jeremy Short, "More Than One Way to Articulate a Vision: A Configurations Approach to Leader Charismatic Rhetoric and Influence." *The Leadership Quarterly*, 27(1) (2018) 156–171. doi:10.1016/j.leaqua.2015.08.002.

26. Becky Smith, "A Case Study of How a Leader's Communication of Organizational Vision Influences the Development of Work Passion" (2017, Order No. 10286682). Available from ProQuest Dissertations & Theses Global (1925954334).

27. Ulrich Jensen, Donald Moynihan, and Heidi Salomonsen, "Communicating the Vision: How Face-to-Face Dialogue Facilitates Transformational Leadership." *Public Administration Review*, 350(3) (2018). doi:10.1111/puar.12922

28. Steffen Strese, Michael Keller, Tessa Flatten, and Malte Brettel, "CEOs' Passion for Inventing and Radical Innovations in SMEs: The Moderating Effect of Shared Vision." *Journal of Small Business Management* 435(3) (2018). doi:10.1111/jsbm.12264

29. Ken Ndalamba, Cam Caldwell, and Verl Anderson, "Leadership Vision as a Moral Duty." *Journal of Management Development* 37(3) (2018) 309–319.

30. Kelly Decker and Ben Decker. "Communicating a Corporate Vision to Your Team." *Harvard Business Review Digital Articles*, 2–5 (2015) 2.

31. Gerard Seijts and Jeffrey Gandz. "Transformational Change and Leader Character." *Business Horizons* 61(2) (2018) 239–249.

32. Shelia Webber and David Webber. "Launching and Leading Intense Teams." *Business Horizons* 58(4) (2015) 449–457.

33. Randall Peterson, "The Vision Thing." *London Business School Review*, 27(2) (2016) 18. doi:10.1111/2057-1615.12112

34. Sarah Bonau, "How to Become an Inspirational Leader, and What to Avoid." *Journal of Management Development*, 36(5) (2017) 614–625. doi:10.1108/JMD-03-2015-0047

35. Dae Chai, Soeg Hwang, and Baek-Kyoo Joo. "Transformational Leadership and Organizational Commitment in Teams: The Mediating Roles of Shared Vision and Team-Goal Commitment." *Performance Improvement Quarterly*, 30(2) (2017) 137–158. doi:10.1002/piq.21244

36. Shelly Kirkpatrick. "Understanding the Role of Vision, Mission, and Values in the HPT Model." *Performance Improvement* 56(3) (2017) 6–14.

37. Michael Mumford, Erin Todd, Cory Higgs, and Tristan McIntosh, "Cognitive Skills and Leadership Performance: The Nine Critical Skills." *Leadership Quarterly* 28(1) (2017) 24. doi:10.1016/j.leaqua.2016.10.012

38. Karl Weick, Kathleen Sutcliffe, and David Obstfeld, "Organizing and the Process of Sensemaking." *Organization Science* 16(4) (2005) 409–421.

39. Margo Brewer, "Exploring the Potential of a Capability Framework as a Vision and "Sensemaking" Tool for Leaders of Interprofessional Education." *Journal of Interprofessional Care* 30(5) (2016) 574–581.

40. Watts, Logan L., Logan M. Steele, and Michael D. Mumford. 2018. "Making Sense of Pragmatic and Charismatic Leadership Stories: Effects on Vision Formation." *The Leadership Quarterly*, September. doi:10.1016/j.leaqua.2018.09.003.

41. Gary Lynn and Faruk Kalay. "The Effect of Vision and Role Clarity on Team Performance." *International Journal of Economic & Administrative Studies* 17 (2016) 175–196.

42. Carmen Mombourquette, "The Role of Vision in Effective School Leadership." *International Studies in Educational Administration (Commonwealth Council for Educational Administration & Management (CCEAM))* 45(1) (2017) 19–36.

43. Susan Ashford, Ned Wellman, Mary Sully De Luque, Katleen De Stobbeleir, and Melody Wollan, "Two Roads to Effectiveness: CEO Feedback Seeking, Vision Articulation, and Firm Performance." *Journal of Organizational Behavior*, 39(1) (2018) 82. doi:10.1002/job.2211

44. Rodney Zemmel, Matt Cuddihy, and Dennis Carey, "How Successful CEOs Manage Their Middle Act." *Harvard Business Review*, 96(3) (2018) 98–105.

45. Maulding Green and Leonard, *Leadership Intelligence*.

46. Wanda S. Maulding Green and Edward E. Leonard, *Improving Your Leadership Intelligence: A Fieldbook for K–12 Leaders*. Lanham, MD: Rowman & Littlefield (2017).

47. Warren Bennis and Robert Thomas, *Geeks and Geezers: How Era, Values, and Defining Moments Shape Leaders*. Boston, MA: Harvard Business School Publishing (2002).

48. Harry Paul, "Recapture Excellence." *TD: Talent Development* 70(11) (2016) 60.

49. Ibid.

50. B. Groysberg, J. Lee, J. Price, and Y. Cheng. "The Leader's Guide to Corporate Culture (Cover Story)." *Harvard Business Review* 96(1) (2018) 44–52.

51. Ian Woodward. "Understanding Values for Insightfully Aware Leadership." *INSEAD Working Papers Collection* Issue 46 (2014) 1–58.

CHAPTER 7

1. D. Watling and T. van Vuren. "The Modelling of Dynamic Route Guidance Systems. Institute of Transport Studies." University of Leeds. Working Paper 341. Retrieved from: http://eprints.whiterose.ac.uk/2224/ 1/ITS246_WP341_uploadable.pdf(1991)

On the one hand, there is static route guidance, which recommends routes on average or expected conditions; although it may recommend different routes at different times of day, it does not respond to traffic conditions actually experienced at that time. On the other hand, in this chapter we shall be concerned only with *dynamic* route guidance (DRG), which bases route recommendations on actual or predicted traffic conditions using data from various detectors in the network, with the recommendations being frequently updated.

DRG systems have the advantage over alternative methods of control mentioned earlier (linked, vehicle-actuated traffic signals or a system of dynamically updated variable message signs) in that they provide the opportunity to influence individual drivers, depending on their own origin and destination and possibly their own route selection criterion. By coordinating the dissemination of the guidance information, such systems are consistent with the current network-wide methods for assessing traditional traffic management measures, in the sense that the control system can help to ensure, to some extent, that any local congestion problem is not simply shifted to another part of the network. The other main advantage of such systems is the possibility for equipped drivers to generate the data on which their routing information is based (through two-way communication links).

2. Daniel Goleman. "What Makes a Leader?" *Harvard Business Review*, 76(6) (1998) 93–102.

3. The concept of alexithymia means dysfunction in emotional awareness, social attachment, and interpersonal relating. Pop-Jordanova and Polenakovic (2014).

4. Annie McKee, "How the Most Emotionally Intelligent CEOs Handle Their Power." *Harvard Business School Cases*, 1 (2016) 2.

5. Simone Phipps, and Leon Prieto, "Why Emotional Intelligence Is Necessary for Effective Leadership: Know the Four Reasons!" *Leadership Excellence Essentials*, 34(6) (2017) 56.

6. Jane McCarroll, "Soft Skills Have Never Been so Important." *NZ Business + Management*, 32(6) (2018) M14–M15.

7. Daniel Goleman and Richard Boyatzis, "Emotional Intelligence Has 12 Elements. Which Do You Need to Work On?" *Harvard Business Review Digital Articles* 2–5 (2017).

8. Tasha Eurich, "Are You a Self-Aware Leader?" Retrieved from http://knowledge.wharton.upenn.edu/article/going-wise-helps-us-make-smarter-decisions/ (2017).

9. Dori Meinert, "Are You an Emotional Genius?" *HR Magazine* 63(2) (2018) 17.

10. Ibid.

11. Eurich "Are You a Self-Aware Leader?"

12. EPSTEIN, A. Build Self-Awareness with Help from Your Team. *Harvard Business Review Digital Articles*, [s. l.], p. 2–4, 2018.

13. Susan David, "How to Manage Your Emotions Without Fighting Them." *Harvard Business Review Digital Articles* 2–4 (2016).

14. Warren Bennis and Robert Thomas. *Geeks and Geezers: How Era, Values, and Defining Moments Shape Leaders.* Boston, MA: Harvard Business School Publishing (2002).

15. Development Dimensions International (DDI), The Conference Board, and EY (2018). Global Leadership Forecast 2018. Retrieved from https://www.ddiworld.com/DDI/media/trend-research/glf2018/global-leadership-forecast-2018_ddi_tr.pdf?ext=.pdf

16. Ibid.

17. Laura-Maija Hero, Eila Lindfors, Vesa Taatila, "Individual Innovation Competence: A Systematic Review and Future Research Agenda." *International Journal of Higher Education*, 6(5) (2017) 103–121.

18. Ibid.

19. Azka Bastaman, Corina Riantoputra, and Eka Gatari, "Do Self-Monitoring and Achievement Orientation Assist or Limit Leader Effectiveness?" In A. A. Ariyanto, H. Muluk, P. Newcombe, F. P. Piercy, E. K. Poerwandari, & S. H. R. Suradijono (Eds.), *Diversity in unity: Perspectives from Psychology and Behavioral Sciences*. New York, NY: Routledge/Taylor & Francis Group (2018) pp. 355–364.

20. Stephanie Ceminsky, *Principal Leadership Behaviors That Influence Teacher Job Satisfaction* (2018, Order No. 10930088). Available from ProQuest Dissertations & Theses Global. (2094858109).

21. Natalie Shefer, Abraham Carmeli, and Ravit Cohen-Meiter, "Bringing Carl Rogers Back in: Exploring the Power of Positive Regard at Work." *British Journal of Management*, 29(1) (2018) 63–68.

22. Annie McKee, "If You Can't Empathize with Your Employees, You'd Better Learn to." *Harvard Business Review Digital Articles*, 2–5 (2016).

23. Ibid.

24. Daniel Goleman (2018, November 17). Daniel Goleman Emotional Intelligence Coaching & Training Programs. https://www.facebook.com/danielgoleman/posts/organizational-awareness-means-being-able/10154747573277978/

25. Ibid.

26. Julie Battilana, and Tiziana Casciaro. "The Network Secrets of Great Change Agents." *Harvard Business Review* 91(7/8) (2013) 62–68.

27. Tiziana Casciaro, Francesca Gino, and Maryam Kouchaki, "Learn to Love Networking." *Harvard Business Review* 94(5) (2016) 104–107.

28. Marko Reimer, Sebastiaan Van Doorn, and Mariano Heyden, "Unpacking Functional Experience Complementarities in Senior Leaders' Influences on CSR Strategy: A CEO-Top Management Team Approach." *Journal of Business Ethics* 151(4) (2018) 977–995.

29. Chase Thiel, Jennifer Griffith, Jay Hardy, David Peterson, and Shane Connelly. "Let's Look at This Another Way: How Supervisors Can Help Subordinates

Manage the Threat of Relationship Conflict." *Journal of Leadership & Organizational Studies* 25(3) (2018) 368–380.

30. Mieke Koeslag-Kreunen, Piet Van den Bossche, Michael Hoven, Marcel Van der Klink, and Wim Gijselaers, "When Leadership Powers Team Learning: A Meta-Analysis." *Small Group Research* 49(4) (2018) 475–513.

31. Eric Garton and Michael Mankins. "Engaging Your Employees Is Good, but Don't Stop There." *Harvard Business Review Digital Articles* 2–6 (2015) 3.

32. Daniel Goleman and M. Lippincott. "Without Emotional Intelligence, Mindfulness Doesn't Work." *Harvard Business School Cases* 1 (2017) 1.

33. Daniel Goleman. "Here's What Mindfulness Is (and Isn't) Good For." *Harvard Business Review Digital Articles* 2–4 (2017) 4.

34. Louis Baron, Véronique Rouleau, Simon Grégoire, and Charles Baron. "Mindfulness and Leadership Flexibility." *Journal of Management Development* 37(2) (2018) 165–177. doi:10.1108/JMD-06-2017-0213.

35. Alison Bacon, Lindsay Lenton-Maughan, and Jon May, "Trait Emotional Intelligence and Social Deviance in Males and Females." *Personality & Individual Differences* 122 (2018) 79–86.

36. Ron Carucci, "Is Your Emotional Intelligence Authentic, or Self-Serving?" *Harvard Business Review Digital Articles* (2018) 2–5.

37. Ibid.

38. Daniel Goleman, "A Sixth Sense for Reading Your Company" (2017). Retrieved from https://www.kornferry.com/institute/organizational-awareness-leadership.

39. Diane Contu. "How Resilience Works." *Harvard Business Review*. Retrieved from: https://hbr.org/2002/05/how-resilience-works (2002).

40. Joshua Margolis and Paul Stoltz. "How to Bounce Back from Adversity." *Harvard Business Review*. Retrieved from: https://hbr.org/2010/01/how-to-bounce-back-from-adversity (2010).

41. Paul Stoltz. "When Adversity Strikes, What Do You Do?" *Harvard Business Review*. Retrieved from: https//hbr.org/2010/07/when-adversity-strikes-what-do-you-do(2010).

42. Robert Thomas. *Crucibles of Leadership: How to Learn from Experience to Become a Great Leader*. Boston, MA: Harvard Business School Publishing Corporation (2008).

43. Daniel Goleman. "Resilience for the Rest of Us." *Harvard Business Review*. Retrieved from: https://hbr.org/2011/04/resilience-for-the-rest-of-us/

44. John Keyser. "Active Listening Leads to Business Success." *T+D*, 67(7) (2013) 26.

45. http://www.thefamouspeople.com/profiles/dwight-david-eisenhower-1270.php

46. Fabio Sala. "Laughing All the Way to the Bank." *Harvard Business Review*. Retrieved from: https://hbr.org/2003/09/laughing-all-the-way-to-the-bank. (2003).

47. Bell Leadership, I. "Bell Leadership Study Finds Humor Gives Leaders the Edge." *Business Wire* (English) (2012).

48. Michael Maccoby. "To Win the Respect of Followers, Leaders Need Personality."

49. Joseph Santora. "Assertiveness and Effective Leadership: Is There a Tipping Point?" *Academy of Management Perspectives*, 21(3) (2007) 84–86.

50. Daniel Ames and Francis J. Flynn. "What Breaks a Leader: The Curvilinear Relation between Assertiveness and Leadership." *Journal of Personality and Social Psychology*, 92 (2007) 307–324.

51. Darren J. Good and Garima Sharma. "A Little More Rigidity: Firming the Construct of Leader Flexibility." *Journal of Change Management* 10(2) (2010) 155–174.

52. Gary Yukl. "The Importance, Assessment, and Development of Flexible Leadership." Practitioner Forum Presented at the 23rd Annual Conference of the Society for Industrial-Organizational Psychology. San Francisco, CA (2008)

53. David Aaker and Briance Mascarenhas. "The Need for Strategic Flexibility." *Journal of Business Strategy* 5(2) (1984) 74.

54. Puina Soffer. "On the Notion of Flexibility in Business Processes." Proceedings of the CAiSE (Conference on Advanced Information Systems Engineering). Porto, Portugal (2005).

55. Daniel Goleman. "Leadership That Gets Results." *Harvard Business Review*, 78(2) (2000) 78–90.

56. Warren Bennis, "Respect and Trust." *Leadership Excellence Essentials*, 31(1) (2014) 11.

CHAPTER 8

1. Warren Bennis. "The Seven Ages of the Leader." *Harvard Business Review*, 82(1) (2004) 46–53.

2. Mary Higgins. *Career Imprints: Creating leaders across an Industry*, 1st ed. San Francisco, CA; Jossey-Bass (2005).

3. Joseph Polizzi and William Frick. "Transformative Preparation and Professional Development: Authentic Reflective Practice for School Leadership." *Teaching & Learning* 26(1) (2012) 20–34.

4. Lynn McAlpin and Cynthia Weston. "Reflection: Issues Related to Improving Professors' Teaching and Students' Learning." *Instructional Science* 28(5–6) (2000) 363–385.

5. Stewart Friedman. *Total Leadership: Be a Better Leader, Have a Richer Life*. Boston, MA: Harvard University Press (2014).

6. Abraham Maslow. "A Theory of Human Motivation." *Psychological Review* 50 (1943) 37–396.

7. Turesky, Elizabeth Fisher; Wood, Diane R. *Academic Leadership* (15337812), 2010, Vol. 8, Issue 3, p. 116–129.

8. Fred A. J. Korthagen. "The Organization in Balance: Reflection and Intuition as Complementary Processes." *Management Learning*, 36(3) (2005) 371–387.

9. Wanda S. Maulding Green and Edward E. Leonard. *Improving Your Leadership Intelligence: A Field Book for K–12 Leaders*. Lanham, MD: Rowman & Littlefield (2017).

CHAPTER 9

1. Lucy Beaumont. "Derailed Leaders." *Training Journal* (2014) 66–69.
2. Center for Creative Leadership "The Bad News: Derailment Happens." Retrieved from: http://www.ccl.org/leadership/pdf/publications/badnewsgoodnews.pdf (2001)
3. Ellen Van Velsor and Evelina Ascalon. "The Role and Impact of Leadership Development in Supporting Ethical Action in Organisations." *Journal of Management Development*, 27(2) (2008) 187–195.
4. Ronald Burke. "Why Leaders Fail: Exploring the Dark Side." *International Journal of Manpower* 27(1) (2006) 91–100.
5. Furnham, Adrian. 2010. *The Elephant in the Boardroom: The Causes of Leadership Derailment*. Basingstoke: Palgrave Macmillan.
6. Ellen Van Velsor and J. B. Leslie. "Why Executives Derail: Perspectives across Time and Cultures." *Academy of Management Executive*, 9(4) (1995) 62–72.
7. Robert Hogan and Joyce Hogan. "Assessing Leadership: A View from the Dark Side." *International Journal of Selection & Assessment*, 9(1/2) (2001) 40.
8. Ibid.
9. Adrian Furnham. "When Leaders Lose the Plot." *Management Today* (2010) 62–66.
10. Adrian Furnham. "Bosses Who Go off the Rails." *Management Today*. Retrieved from http://www.managementtoday.co.uk/features/1004503/bosses-who-go-off-the-rails/(2010).
11. Ibid.
12. The following sources support the information of the Five Factor Model. Bart Wille and Filip. De Fruyt, "Fifty Shades of Personality: Integrating Five-Factor Model Bright and Dark Sides of Personality at Work." *Industrial and Organizational Psychology: Perspectives on Science and Practice*, 7(1) (2017) 121–126; Eamonn Ferguson, Heather Semper, Janet Yates, Edward Fitzgerald, Anya Skatova, and David James, "The 'Dark Side' and 'Bright Side' of Personality: When Too Much Conscientiousness and Too Little Anxiety Are Detrimental with Respect to the Acquisition of Medical Knowledge and Skill." *PLoS ONE*, 9(2) (2014) 1–11; Adrain Furnham, and John Crump. "A Big Five Facet Analysis of Sub-Clinical Narcissism: Understanding Boldness in Terms of Well-Known Personality Traits." *Personality and Mental Health* 8(3) (2014) 209–217; Oluf Gøtzsche-Astrup, and Adrain Furnham. "The Relationship between Bright- and Dark-Side Personality Traits." *Personality and Individual Differences* 87 (2015) 206–211; Peter Harms, and Seth Spain. "Beyond the Bright Side: Dark Personality at Work." *Applied Psychology: An International Review* 64(1) (2015) 15–24; Reece Akhtar, Chris Humphreys, and Adrain Furnham, "Exploring the Relationships among Personality, Values, and Business Intelligence." *Consulting Psychology Journal: Practice and Research* 67(3) (2015) 258–276; Malgorzata Sobol-Kwapinska, "Positive Orientation: Exploring the Factors That Constitute the Bright Side of Personality." *Social Behavior & Personality: An International Journal* 44(10) (2016) 1613–1618; Adrain Furnham, Luke Treglown, Gillian Hyde, and Geoff Trickey, "The Bright and Dark Side of Altruism: Demographic, Personality Traits,

and Disorders Associated with Altruism." *Journal of Business Ethics* 134(3) (2016) 359–368; Adrain Furnham. "Personality Differences in Managers Who Have, and Have Not, Worked Abroad." *European Management Journal* 35(1) (2017) 39–45; Adrain Furnham and John Crump. "Personality Correlates of Passive-Aggressiveness: A NEO-PI-R Domain and Facet Analysis of the HDS Leisurely Scale." *Journal of Mental Health* 26(6) (2017) 496–501; Judith Volmer, Iris Koch, and Anja Göritz, "The Bright and Dark Sides of Leaders Dark Triad traits: Effects on Subordinates' Career Success and Well-being': Corrigendum." *Personality and Individual Differences* 108 (2017) 226; Adrain Furnham. "The Bright and Dark Side of Achievement Motivation." *Current Psychology: A Journal for Diverse Perspectives on Diverse Psychological Issues* (2018); Dominik Paleczek, Sabine Bergner, and Robert Rybnicek. "Predicting Career Success: Is the Dark Side of Personality Worth Considering?" *Journal of Managerial Psychology* 33(6) (2018) 437–456; Oluf Gøtzsche-Astrup. "The Bright and Dark Sides of Talent at Work: A Study of the Personalities of Talent-Development-Program Participants." *Consulting Psychology Journal: Practice and Research* 70(2) (2018) 167–181.

13. American Psychiatric Association. (2013). *Diagnostic and Statistical Manual of Mental Disorder*, 5th ed. (DSM-5). Arlington, VA: American Psychiatric Association.

14. Robert Hogan, and Robert Kaiser. "What We Know about Leadership." *Review of General Psychology* 9(2) (2005) 169–180.

15. Jason Pierce and Herman Aguinis, "The Too-Much-of-a-Good-Thing Effect in Management." *Journal of Management*, 39(2) (2013) 313–338.

16. Ibid.

17. DSM-5.

18. Derek Lusk and Tomas Chamorro-Premuzic. "The Dark Side of Resilience. *Harvard Business School Cases* 1 (2017).

19. Lewis Garrad and Tomas Chamorro-Premuzic. "The Dark Side of High Employee Engagement." *Harvard Business Review Digital Articles* 2–4 (2016).

20. Zheng Xiaotao, Xiaoling Yang, Ismael Diaz, and Mingchuan Yu. "Is Too Much Inclusive Leadership a Good Thing? An Examination of Curvilinear Relationship between Inclusive Leadership and Employees' Task Performance." *International Journal of Manpower* 39(7) (2018) 882–895.

21. Guiquan Li, Alex Rubenstein, Weipeng Lin, Mo Wang, and Xingwen Chen. "The Curvilinear Effect of Benevolent Leadership on Team Performance: The Mediating Role of Team Action Processes and the Moderating Role of Team Commitment." *Personnel Psychology* 71(3) (2018) 369–397.

22. Adrain Furnham, Luke Treglown, Gillian Hyde, and Geoff Trickey. "The Bright and Dark Side of Altruism: Demographic, Personality Traits, and Disorders Associated with Altruism." *Journal of Business Ethics* 134(3) (2016) 359–368.

23. Tomas Chamorro-Premuzic. "Could Your Personality Derail Your Career? Don't Take These Traits to the Extreme." *Harvard Business Review* 95(5) (2017) 138–141.

24. Ibid.

25. Jonathan Gottschall, "Theranos and the Dark Side of Storytelling." *Harvard Business School Cases* 1 (2016).

26. Jasmine Vergauwe, Bart Wille, Joeri Hofmans, Robert Kaiser, and Filip De Fruyt. "Too Much Charisma Can Make Leaders Look Less Effective." *Harvard Business Review Digital Articles* 2–6 (2017).

27. Joshua Miller, Chelsea Sleep, and Donald Lynam. "DSM-5 Alternative Model of Personality Disorder: Testing the Trait Perspective Captured in Criterion B." *Current Opinion in Psychology* 21 (2018) 50–54.

28. Nadine Page, Sabine Bergner, and Stefan Wills. "Who Empathizes with Machiavellian or Narcissistic Leaders?" *Harvard Business School Cases* 1 (2017) 2.

29. Carrie Blair, Katherine Helland, and Bill Walton. "Leaders Behaving Badly: The Relationship between Narcissism and Unethical Leadership." *Leadership & Organization Development Journal* 38(2) (2017) 333–346. doi:10.1108/LODJ-09-2015-0209

30. Hillary DeShong, Ashley Helle, Gregory Lengel, Neil Meyer, and Stephanie Mulins-Sweatt. "Facets of the Dark Triad: Utilizing the Five-Factor Model to Describe Machiavellianism." *Personality and Individual Differences* 105 (January 15, 2017) 218–223. doi:10.1016/j.paid.2016.09.053.

31. Peter Muris, Harald Merckelbach, Henry Otgaar, and Ewout Meijer. "The Malevolent Side of Human Nature: A Meta-Analysis and Critical Review of the Literature on the Dark Triad (Narcissism, Machiavellianism, and Psychopathy)." *Perspectives on Psychological Science* 12(2) (2017) 183–204.

32. Adrain. Furnham, Steven Richards, DelRoy Paulhus. "The Dark Triad of Personality: A 10-Year Review." *Social and Personality Psychology Compass* 7(3) (2013) 199–216.

33. J. Birkinshaw and M. Haas, "Increase Your Return on Failure." *Harvard Business Review* 94(5) (2016) 88–93.

34. Chamorro-Premuzic. "Could Your Personality Derail Your Career?"

35. D. Meinert. "Why Leaders Fail: Learn to Course-Correct before Your Career Founders." *HR Magazine* 62(8) (2017) 18.

36. Ellen Van Velsor and Evelina Ascalon. "The Role and Impact of Leadership Development in Supporting Ethical Action in Organisations." *Journal of Management Development*, 27(2) (2008) 187–195.

37. Bill George. "Why Leaders Lose Their Way." *Harvard Business School Working Knowledge*. Retrieved from: https://hbr.org/2011/06/why-leaders-lose-their-way (2011).

CHAPTER 10

1. Warren Bennis. "The Seven Ages of the Leader." *Harvard Business Review* 82(1) (2004) 46–53.

2. Joseph Polizzi and William Frick. "Transformative Preparation and Professional Development: Authentic Reflective Practice for School Leadership."

3. John Kotter. "The Leadership Factor." *McKinsey Quarterly*. Issue 2 (1988) 71–78.

4. Ibid.

5. John Baldoni. "Leader's Credibility Is Golden." *Harvard Business Review*. Retrieved from: https://hbr.org/2008/11/leaders-credibility-is-golden (2008).

6. Ibid.

7. Frederick Dembowski. "The Changing Roles of Leadership and Management in Educational Administration." National Council of Professor of Educational Administration (NCPEA) (2006).

8. Daniel Goleman. "What Makes a Leader?" *Harvard Business Review*, 76(6) (1998) 93–102.

9. Nancy Koehn, "The Leadership Journey of Abraham Lincoln." *Mckinsey Quarterly* 2 (2018) 77–87.

10. Ibid, p. 3.

11. Ibid.

12. Ibid.

13. Ibid.

14. Ibid.

About the Authors

Wanda S. Maulding Green is an educational leadership faculty member at the University of South Alabama and has served in leadership roles in both K–12 and higher education. She is currently a leadership trainer and coach for K–12 and higher education practitioners.

Edward E. Leonard is a retired school superintendent and higher education administrator. He currently teaches leadership courses at William Carey University and is a trainer and leadership coach for persons in both K–12 and higher education.

www.ingramcontent.com/pod-product-compliance
Lightning Source LLC
Chambersburg PA
CBHW021845220426
43663CB00005B/417